COLOMBIAN LABYRINTH

The Synergy of Drugs and Insurgency and Its Implications for Regional Stability

Angel Rabasa **Peter Chalk**

Prepared for the United States Air Force

Project AIR FORCE

RAND

The research reported here was sponsored by the United States Air Force under Contract F49642-01-C-0003. Further information may be obtained from the Strategic Planning Division, Directorate of Plans, Hq USAF.

Library of Congress Cataloging-in-Publication Data

Rabasa, Angel.
    Columbian labyrinth : the synergy of drugs and insurgency and its implications
for regional stability / Angel M. Rabasa, Peter Chalk.
      p. cm.
    "MR-1339."
    Includes bibliographical references.
    ISBN 0-8330-2994-0
    1. National security—Colombia. 2. Colombia—Strategic aspects. 3. National
security—Latin America. 4. Colombia—Politics and government—1974– 5.
Insurgency—Colombia—History—20th century. 6. Guerrillas—Colombia—
History—20th century. 7. Drug traffic—Colombia—History—20th century. 8.
United States—Military relations—Colombia. 9. Colombia—Military relations—
United States. I. Chalk, Peter. II. Title.

UA625 .R33 2001
986.106'35—dc21

                           2001031639

RAND is a nonprofit institution that helps improve policy and decisionmaking through research and analysis. RAND® is a registered trademark. RAND's publications do not necessarily reflect the opinions or policies of its research sponsors.

Published 2001 by RAND
1700 Main Street, P.O. Box 2138, Santa Monica, CA 90407-2138
1200 South Hayes Street, Arlington, VA 22202-5050
201 North Craig Street, Suite 102, Pittsburgh, PA 15213-1516
RAND URL: http://www.rand.org/
To order RAND documents or to obtain additional information,
contact Distribution Services: Telephone: (310) 451-7002;
Fax: (310) 451-6915; Internet: order@rand.org

Drug trafficking and political disintegration in Colombia could confront the United States, if present trends continue, with the most serious foreign and security policy crisis in the Western Hemisphere since the Central American wars of the 1980s. The first question is why Colombia matters. U.S. policy toward Colombia has been driven to a large extent by counter-narcotics considerations, but the situation in that South American country is a national security as much as a drug policy problem. Colombia is a strategically important country. It is South America's fourth largest country in area and the second largest in population. It is the only South American country with coastlines on both the Atlantic and Pacific oceans and it is contiguous to the Caribbean basin, Central America, Venezuela and its oil fields, and Panama and the Canal. Colombia also has some of the largest untapped petroleum reserves in the Western Hemisphere. Colombia's trajectory will also influence the direction of broader trends in the unstable Andean region and beyond.

This study, conducted in Project AIR FORCE's Strategy and Doctrine Program, examines

- the sources of instability in Colombia;

- the objectives, strategies, strengths, and weaknesses of the major Colombian actors—government, guerrillas, and paramilitaries—and the balance of forces among them; and

- the impact of the U.S. assistance program.

The study concludes with possible scenarios for Colombia and the implications of these scenarios for the security and stability of neighboring states and U.S. regional security interests.

This research was sponsored by the Deputy Chief of Staff for Air and Space Operations, U.S. Air Force (AF/XO), and the Director of Strategic Planning, U.S. Air Force (AF/XPX). It is part of a larger study, entitled "New Challenges for the U.S. Air Force," that reviews "off-baseline" scenarios and threats—those receiving little attention in the defense community—for the purpose of identifying weak links in potential U.S. Air Force operations. Concurrent research is examining potential vulnerabilities and remedies in the deployment and employment of aerospace forces.

This report should be of value to the national security community and interested members of the general public, especially those with an interest in Latin America and the future of hemispheric relations. Comments are welcome and should be sent to the authors or to the project leader, David Shlapak. Research was completed in January 2001.

PROJECT AIR FORCE

Project AIR FORCE, a division of RAND, is the United States Air Force's Federally Funded Research and Development Center (FFRDC) for studies and analyses. It provides the Air Force with independent analyses of policy alternatives affecting the development, employment, combat readiness, and support of current and future aerospace forces. Research is performed in four programs: Aerospace Force Development; Manpower, Personnel, and Training; Resource Management; and Strategy and Doctrine.

CONTENTS

FIGURES

TABLES

SUMMARY

Current instability in Colombia derives from the interaction and resulting synergies stemming from two distinct tendencies: the development of an underground criminal drug economy and the growth of armed challenges to the state's authority. The first source of instability is reflected in the increasingly pervasive influence of drug networks and their infiltration of key societal institutions; the second is the growth of guerrilla armies as well as the development of organized violence perpetrated by illegal self-defense forces, also known as paramilitaries. The actions of drug traffickers, guerrillas, and paramilitaries have exacerbated deeper problems in Colombian society: the central government's loss of authority, economic deterioration, and social disintegration.

The synergy of which the title of this report speaks occurs because the strength of the guerrillas (particularly the largest group, the Revolutionary Armed Forces of Colombia, known by its Spanish acronym, FARC) is directly linked to the guerrillas' control of drug-producing and drug-processing areas. Income from drug trafficking and other illegal activities provides the FARC with the resources to intensify its political and military challenge to the Colombian state.[1] This synergy of drugs and insurgency has generated a new kind of security

---

[1]To some degree, the Colombian situation can be understood as part of a category of civil conflicts that has recently come to the attention of scholars: insurgencies that derive their political and military strength from access to revenues from export commodities—in the case of Colombia, drugs. See Paul Collier and Anke Hoeffler, "Justice-Seeking and Loot-Seeking in Civil War," presentation to World Bank workshop, Washington, D.C., 1999.

threat—neither an old-fashioned insurgency nor a simple criminal cartel, but a threat that incorporates elements and strengths of both.

From the standpoint of Colombia's security, this threat is primarily political and military. For the FARC leadership, funding from the illegal drug traffic is a means to an end, not an end in itself. The end is political power. It follows that solutions that address the problem as one of countering criminal activity rather than a political-military challenge to the state are likely to miss the target.

The policy problem, for both Colombia and the United States, is that, publicly at least, "Plan Colombia," the Bogotá government's blueprint for restoring stability, and U.S. support for it, are predicated on a doubtful strategy. The strategy gives pride of place to moving against the drug producers and traffickers, on the argument that drying up funding from drugs will undermine the guerrillas' strength. Yet it is far from certain that the strategy will succeed. The guerrillas have other sources of financing, and the illegal drug trade has demonstrated the capacity to adapt and adjust to counter-narcotics strategies. Nor, based on historical experience, is it clear that alternative sources of income for coca farmers can be developed very soon. In these circumstances, moving against the drug-producing areas could have the effect of increasing support for the guerrillas among those who stand to lose their livelihood.

The contraction of the Colombian government's authority has significant implications for regional stability. There has already been a spillover of the armed conflict in Colombia into neighboring states. Colombia's neighbors fear that they are caught between a hammer and an anvil. They are concerned that if Colombia and its allies move aggressively against the drug-producing areas in southern Colombia, traffickers and guerrillas would look for sanctuaries and bases of operations across Colombia's borders. Conversely, if security conditions in Colombia deteriorate further, the regional reverberations could be much worse.

THE ILLEGAL DRUG TRADE AND U.S. COUNTER-NARCOTICS POLICY

For the past two decades, U.S. policy toward Colombia has been dominated by efforts to stem the flow of cocaine and, more recently, heroin, from the Andean region of South America to the United States. In the early 1990s, the focus of U.S. counter-narcotics policy shifted from interdicting illegal drugs from Mexican and Caribbean transit zones to attacking the production and refining at the source in Peru, Bolivia, and Colombia. There have been increasing indications, however, that this approach has not succeeded in reducing the drug problem. Since 1995 the area under coca cultivation in Colombia has expanded by over 140 percent. The large drug cartels that dominated the cocaine trade in the early 1990s have been replaced by groupings that are flatter, less hierarchical, and more diversified, and hence harder to penetrate. Moreover, disruption of the so-called air bridge connecting coca growers in Bolivia and Peru with refiners in Colombia has impelled traffickers to integrate production closer to home, so that most of the coca used for cocaine production is now grown in Colombia. In addition, traffickers have diversified into heroin production from poppies also grown in Colombia.

INSURGENCY AND POLITICAL VIOLENCE

Over the same period (1980s to the present), guerrilla activity has dramatically expanded. From ambushes and small-scale attacks, the guerrillas, particularly the FARC, moved to multicolumn operations involving hundreds of fighters. At the same time, the guerrillas expanded their area of operations from their original base areas in thinly populated, inhospitable regions on Colombia's periphery to densely populated and economically strategic areas closer to Colombia's major cities. Both the FARC and the smaller National Liberation Army (ELN) have demonstrated the capacity to cut off land communications between major cities and to disrupt the country's electrical and petroleum infrastructure almost at will. Over the last five years, the FARC has established new fronts on the eastern cordillera of the Andes, bringing it closer to Bogotá and giving it control of poppy-growing areas and a stake in the growing heroin trade.

The Pastrana government's hopes for restoring peace rest in the success of negotiations with the guerrillas. To demonstrate its good faith, Bogotá conceded to the FARC effective control of a "demilitarized zone" of some 42,000 square kilometers in south-central Colombia. This "state within the state" constitutes a major strategic asset for the FARC. The FARC uses this sanctuary as a base for launching operations, resting and refitting its forces, moving and refining drugs, stockpiling arms, and even holding prisoners and hostages. As of this writing, the Colombian government was considering the establishment of a smaller demilitarized zone for the ELN in the middle Magdalena valley.

Despite these concessions by the Colombian government, the question remains whether the FARC really wants a peace settlement. In Guatemala, El Salvador, and other cases, the key to a settlement was the agreement of the rebel forces to demobilize in exchange for guarantees of personal security and participation in a democratic political process. The guerrillas in those countries agreed to these arrangements when they had been essentially defeated (Guatemala) or had come to realize that a military victory was not possible (El Salvador). In Colombia, by contrast, the guerrillas have not been defeated, and the military situation is far too fluid to be considered a stalemate.

At the same time, both the government and the FARC have an interest in continuing the negotiations, even if conditions for a peace settlement are not present. The government has staked its credibility on the negotiating track and hopes that the negotiations will develop a momentum that will enmesh the FARC in the process. For its part, the FARC derives substantial advantages from the talks. The negotiations enhance its domestic and international stature and legitimacy and, by sanctioning the continued operation of the "demilitarized zone," the negotiating arrangements give the FARC some real strategic and operational advantages.

The third party in Colombia's three-sided civil war is the *autodefensas,* the illegal self-defense forces, also known as paramilitaries. These groups, organized under an umbrella organization, the United Self-Defense Forces of Colombia (AUC), initially emerged in reaction to guerrilla violence. They are particularly active in areas where the state has lost the capacity to provide security to the population. The AUC has committed egregious human rights violations and is increasingly involved in the drug trade. Yet, its numbers have continued to grow and its forces have succeeded in displacing the guerrillas from a number of contested areas.

For the Colombian government, the dilemma is whether to treat the illegal self-defense groups as political actors, and thus as legitimate participants in the peace negotiations, or as criminals to be suppressed. Colombian public opinion is divided on the matter, and so far the government has taken the second track. Nevertheless, whether accepted as legitimate political actors or not, these groups have become another power center challenging the state's already frayed authority. Realistically, because the paramilitaries are the product of an environment of insecurity, they will continue to be a factor in Colombia's crisis as long as the conditions that gave rise to them are not changed. An alternative approach could be to establish a network of government-supervised self-defense organizations. Legalized self-defense units could at least give the central government more control over their activities, and possibly improve the prospects for peace by empowering local communities to provide for their own security.

The Colombian military suffered devastating defeats at the hands of the FARC from 1996 to 1998 and is now trying hard to adapt and modernize. New operational and tactical approaches have produced some improved results, especially in an increased tempo of counter-insurgency actions. This said, the armed forces have not yet developed the capability to control the guerrillas, let alone defeat them. Indeed, while the military has the advantage in numbers and fire-power, for the most part the guerrillas maintain the operational and tactical initiative.

PLAN COLOMBIA AND IMPLICATIONS FOR U.S. DEFENSE PLANNING

Plan Colombia, the Colombian government's response to the crisis, incorporates elements of a national strategy to reverse the downside trends and reestablish its authority in areas controlled or contested by guerrillas and other non-state actors. However, there is criticism that the Colombian government strategy derives less from an analysis of the situation in Colombia than from U.S. political constraints that can justify aid only in terms of counter-narcotics assistance. Moreover, the Colombian government's political strategy relies on the success of the peace negotiations—a problematic prospect—and lacks a clear link to well-defined political-military goals.

Aside from strategic clarity, the Colombian government needs to develop adequate implementation instrumentalities. Developing a capable military force will require a thoroughgoing military reform, including implementation of the Colombian High Command's goal of replacing conscripts—who currently constitute 70 percent of the military personnel—with an all-volunteer force, and remedying weaknesses in mobility, intelligence, and communications. Also, the police and military operations in counter-narcotics and counter-insurgency efforts need to be better integrated.

All of this will require adequate funding. The proportion of gross domestic product (GDP) (3.56 percent) that Colombia spends on defense and security has not changed much since the early 1990s. That figure is higher than the average for Latin America, but far too low for a country fighting an active insurgency. Colombia has critical unmet needs in the social and economic spheres, but there are irreducible military requirements that will have to be met if the Colombian government is to restore a climate of security that is a prerequisite for economic and social recovery.

The United States recognizes the nexus between the guerrillas and the drug traffic, but sees the problem as essentially one of counter-narcotics policy. As a result, U.S. efforts are focused on strengthening Colombian anti-narcotics capabilities while insisting that U.S. military assistance is not directed against the guerrillas themselves. U.S. policy therefore misses the point that the political and military control that the guerrillas exercise over an ever-larger part of Colombia's territory and population is at the heart of their challenge to the Bogotá government's authority. The United States ought to rethink whether this distinction between counter-narcotics and counter-insurgency can be sustained, and whether Colombia and its allies can be successful in the war against drugs if the Colombian government fails to regain control of its territory.

By taking the lead in mustering international support for Plan Colombia, the United States has raised its stake in the success of the Colombian government's strategy. If that strategy falters, the United States would be confronted with the choice of either escalating its commitment or scaling it down. The latter option would involve a significant loss of credibility and a degradation of the United States' ability to protect its interests in this critical region. To avoid this outcome, the United States would have to provide sustained support until the Colombian government regains the political and military initiative.

To help Colombia improve its conventional military capabilities, the first priority is to develop new concepts of operations to detect, identify, and attack light infantry (guerrilla) targets. Air-land synergies, which the Colombian military has employed in encounters since 1998, have proven effective in countering the guerrilla tactic of massing to attack isolated government positions or units. To do still better will require improved intelligence on the type, location, and activities of the adversary. Newly developed platforms, sensors, weapons, and analytic tools could be brought to bear as well. No less important is awareness of the vulnerabilities of air-land strategies. In the battle of Dabeida (see Chapter Four), the guerrillas' ability to interfere with the helicopters that the Colombian military relies on for air mobility left government forces dangerously exposed.

The United States should also assist the Colombian government in regaining control of the major roads and the 18,000 kilometers of navigable rivers that serve as highways for guerrillas and drug traffickers. Road and river control can go a long way in helping the Colombian government establish a "bubble of security" that is necessary for other activities—such as civil affairs and economic and social reconstruction—to proceed.

The second prong of a proactive U.S. strategy is to work with concerned Latin American countries to contain the threat of spillover and regional destabilization. The United States should explore ways of helping countries such as Panama and Ecuador regain control of their borders with Colombia. Shutting down to the extent possible the narcotraffickers' and guerrillas' pipeline is critical to the success of any strategy. At the same time, the United States should start to lay the groundwork for a multilateral inter-American response in the event that the crisis in Colombia intensifies and spills beyond its borders.

There are significant operational-level implications for the U.S. Air Force, which are being documented in another report. The turnover of Howard Air Force Base to Panama in 1999 deprived the United States of its most important air base south of the continental United

States. None of the operating facilities used by the United States for the counter-narcotics mission (Curacao and Aruba; Manta, Ecuador; and Comalapa, El Salvador) has the geographic advantages of the former Howard air base in Panama. Although the condition of the base and political sensitivities preclude a return to Howard at this time, the infrequently used cargo runway at Tocumen airport near Panama City is an option that could be explored with the Panamanian government.

In conclusion, understanding the Colombian labyrinth drives home the realization that drugs and insurgency are intertwined in complicated and changing ways, but the former cannot be addressed without dealing with the latter. This argues for improving Colombia's capabilities, especially in the military sphere. At the same time, the United States needs to work with Colombia's neighbors to contain the spillover of the drug trade and the civil conflict in Colombia and the risk of regional destabilization.

ACKNOWLEDGMENTS

The authors wish to thank, first of all, our colleagues in the RAND Project AIR FORCE project "New Challenges for the U.S. Air Force," especially David Shlapak, David Thaler, and Dan Fox. Their contribution to the development of this study, particularly in crisis gaming and analysis of operational issues, was invaluable. We also wish to thank Zalmay Khalilzad, the former director of the Strategy and Doctrine Program, under whose auspices this study was initiated, his successor, Ted Harshberger, and the reviewers of this manuscript, Greg Treverton of RAND and David Spencer of the Center for Naval Analyses. Dr. Treverton's comments helped to sharpen the focus of the analysis and add depth to the study, and Mr. Spencer contributed invaluable insights into the strategy and tactics of the parties in the Colombian conflict.

Our most important sources for the study were Colombian military authorities and defense academics, who provided critical data and insights. We thank in particular the embassy and office of the defense attaché of Colombia in Washington; the *Comandancia General* (General Staff) of the Colombian armed forces; Dr. Francisco Leal Buitrago, dean of the faculty of Political Sciences at the Universidad de los Andes; Dr. Alfredo Rangel, Colombia's leading politico-military analyst; Dr. Camilo Echandía, the author of the most complete statistical survey of the violence in Colombia; and Panamian defense expert Dr. Jorge Aparicio. We also thank the ambassadors of Venezuela and Panama to the United States, the Venezuelan Armed Force and the Institute of Higher National Defense Studies of Venequela, and the National Police, Air Service, and Naval Service of Panama for their cooperation with the research for this study. We are grateful to Dr. Fernando Carrillo of the Inter-American Development Bank; Professor Malcolm Deas of St. Antony's College, Oxford University; and Dr. Bruce M. Bagley of the University of Miami for sharing their views on Colombia and the region.

Finally, our assistant, Joanna Alberdeston, and our editors, Jeanne Heller and Christopher Kelly, deserve credit for their help in the preparation of the manuscript for publication.

AUC   Autodefensas Unidas de Colombia (United Self-Defense Forces of Colombia)

CGSB   Coordinadora Guerrillera Simón Bolívar (Simón Bolívar Guerrilla Coordinator)

ELN   Ejército de Liberación Nacional (National Liberation Army)

EPL   Ejército Popular de Liberación (People's Liberation Army)

ERG   Ejército Revolucionario Guevarista (Guevarist Revolutionary Army)

ERP   Ejército Revolucionario del Pueblo (People's Revolutionary Army)

FARC   Fuerzas Armadas Revolucionarias de Colombia (Revolutionary Armed Forces of Colombia)

FMLN   Frente Farabundo Martí para la Liberación Nacional (Farabundo Marti National Liberation Front, El Salvador)

M-19   Movimiento Revolucionario 19 de Abril (19th of April Revolutionary Movement, Colombia)

URNG   Unidad Revolucionaria Nacional Guatemalteca (Guatemalan National Revolutionary United Front)

Chapter One

INTRODUCTION: SOURCES OF INSTABILITY

The current instability in Colombia derives from the interaction and resulting synergies of an underground criminal drug economy and the growth of armed challenges to the state's authority. The first source of instability is reflected in the pervasive influence of drug networks and their infiltration of key societal institutions; the second lies in the growth of guerrilla armies, paramilitaries, and "privatized" security forces. The confluence of these factors has exacerbated even deeper problems in Colombian society, including the loss of central government authority, economic deterioration, and social disinte- gration, and may be creating the conditions for a "failed state." A failed state is characterized by a severe political crisis in which the institutions of the central government are so weakened that they can no longer maintain authority or political order beyond the major cities and sometimes not even there.[1]

U.S. policy has focused its attention on the counter-narcotics effort, with indifferent success. However, the narcotics and insurgency problems are intertwined and growing even more so, so that effec- tively dealing with one will likely involve dealing with the other. Therefore, U.S. policy needs to be informed by a better understand- ing of the complexities of the Colombian situation and U.S. military planners should consider the consequences of being drawn deeper into the "Colombian labyrinth."

---

[1]See Daniel C. Esty, Jack Goldstone, Ted Robert Gurr, Barbara Harff, Pamela Surko, Alan N. Unger, and Robert S. Chen, "The State Failure Project: Early Warning Research for U.S. Foreign Policy Planning," in John L. Davies and Ted Robert Gurr (eds.), *Pre- ventive Measures: Building Risk Assessment and Crisis Early Warning Systems* (1998).

This study analyzes the sources of instability in Colombia: the decay of government authority and social cohesion and the development of parallel economic, political, and military structures. State failure, of course, is measured on a continuum, in that few states in less-developed countries have complete control of their territory and functions. The issue is how advanced is the decay of Colombian political and social institutions and whether the Colombian state is in danger of collapse or of being deposed by other forces. To this end, the study seeks to examine the direction of economic, social, political, and military trends in Colombia and identify possible outcomes and their implications for regional stability and U.S. security interests.

POLITICAL TRENDS

Colombia historically has been a weak state, exercising only incomplete jurisdiction over its territory and only imperfectly able to enforce its authority over powerful corporate or local interests. According to Colombian political scientist Francisco Leal Buitrago, lack of national integration and a large degree of regional autonomy have characterized the Colombian political environment. None of Colombia's regions has been strong enough to dominate the others; as a result, a dominant center has not emerged. Bogotá is the political, but not the economic, capital of Colombia. Since the late 19th century, Medellín has been the dynamic center of economic activity; other economic and political centers have developed on the Atlantic coast and the Cauca Valley. The forces at play in the Colombian conflict reflect this fragmentation; none is strong enough to decisively defeat the others.[2]

The response of governments in Bogotá to the state's weakness has been to conciliate, negotiate with, or, if possible, ignore challengers, rather than to try to impose its authority. As discussed in more detail in Chapter Seven, a series of negotiations, some successful and some not, have punctuated the history of the Colombian authorities' dealing with rebels of various stripes.

In addition to its inherent weakness, the Colombian government suffered a severe loss of legitimacy and international support after

---

[2]Conversation with Francisco Leal Buitrago, Bogotá, April 2000.

revelations of drug network financing of the successful presidential campaign of Liberal Party candidate Ernesto Samper in 1994. The subsequent decision by the Clinton administration not to certify that Colombia was cooperating against the drug trade resulted in the freezing of U.S. assistance to Colombia except for counter-narcotics purposes.[3]

The 1998 election brought to power a coalition of Conservatives and dissident Liberals headed by Andrés Pastrana, the son of a former president. The Pastrana government regained much of the international and domestic standing that had been lost by the preceding administration. A major asset was renewed strong support by the United States. Nevertheless, the Pastrana administration has not been able to make discernable headway in strengthening the state.

The Pastrana administration staked a great deal of its credibility on the negotiation of a peace agreement with the country's major guerrilla organization, the Revolutionary Armed Forces of Colombia (FARC). In November 1998, within four months of his inauguration, the President withdrew Colombian military forces from a 42,139 square kilometer "demilitarized zone" (*zona de despeje*) in south central Colombia, which the FARC demanded as a condition for negotiations. Although the idea of negotiations enjoyed considerable support, Pastrana's approach entailed substantial political costs, including the resignation of Defense Minister Rodrigo Lloreda in May 1999, and stresses between the government and the military. Lloreda objected to the negotiating approach articulated by Pastrana's negotiator, which implied the indefinite FARC control of the *zona de despeje*. Despite government concessions, the FARC continued the attacks on government and infrastructure targets, kidnappings, and other acts of violence and disruption.

The lack of results of the negotiation strategy has led to a sharp loss of public confidence in President Pastrana.[4] The Pastrana adminis-

---

[3]Certification is an annual congressionally mandated process in which the U.S. President certifies that foreign countries are cooperating in counter-narcotics efforts (see Chapter Two).

[4]According to a Centro Nacional de Consultoría (CNC) poll in August 2000, only 23 percent of the respondents approved of Pastrana's administration, while 71 percent disapproved and the rest had no opinion. Seventy-nine percent believed that the peace process was going badly. www.cnccol.com. Pastrana's approval rate rose to 52

tration, moreover, became embroiled in a debilitating struggle with the Liberal Party majority in the Congress in the spring of 2000. The President called for a referendum to restructure and reduce the size of the Congress; the congressional opposition threatened to revoke Pastrana's mandate. The political power struggle blocked economic reforms approved by the International Monetary Fund (IMF) and was a factor in the downgrading of Colombia's long-term foreign debt rating by Standard & Poor's and other international rating services.[5]

ECONOMIC TRENDS

The stress on Colombia's political and social institutions was compounded by the country's deepest economic crisis in 50 years. The downturn in the Colombian economy was a sharp reversal from the record of the previous half-century. Colombia historically has had one of the most stable economies in Latin America. The economy enjoyed uninterrupted growth from 1932 until the mid-1990s—an exceptional performance even by the standards of developed countries. During the 1980s, the so-called lost decade of Latin America, the Colombian economy grew at an average annual rate of 3.5 percent and was the only major Latin American country not to restructure its foreign debt during the Latin American debt crisis.

The exceptional performance of the Colombian economy resulted from a diversified economic base and responsible macroeconomic management. Until the 1960s, the growth of the Colombian economy, including the development of the industrial sector, was linked to the export of coffee, which represented 60 percent of the value of Colombia's exports in 1970. In the 1960s, Colombia, like most other Latin American countries in this period, tried to develop the industrial sector through a policy of import substitution. Internal markets, however, proved to be inadequate to support economic expansion and the country adopted a mixed model of economic development—

---

percent in February 2001, after the resumption of the peace negotiations with the FARC, which had been suspended by the FARC in November 2000 because of the government's alleged failure to combat the country's paramilitary groups. *Cambio*, February 19–26, 2001.

[5]"Colombian Turmoil, S&P Downgrade Add to Currency Woes," *The Wall Street Journal*, May 25, 2000.

a policy of promoting non-traditional exports but without completely dismantling the structure of protectionist tariff barriers. The López Michelsen administration (1974–1978) set for itself the ambitious goal of turning Colombia into the Japan of Latin America, although the need to stabilize public finances forced it to give priority to reducing the deficit and fighting inflation.[6]

Economic policy in the first half of the 1990s was based on setting targets for inflation, reducing the fiscal deficit, and decreasing the deficit in the trade and current account balance. There was a small fiscal deficit (under 0.5 percent of gross domestic product [GDP]) in 1992, small surpluses in 1991 and 1993, and a 2.5 percent surplus in 1994. In 1990, the Barco administration began a process of liberalization and privatization of the economy known as the *apertura* (opening), which was continued and accelerated by the Gaviria administration (1990–1994). The principal objective of the opening was to remove protectionist obstacles to the growth of the export sector. The Gaviria administration also implemented structural reforms, including adoption of a new constitution and tax reform. The economy responded by growing at a rate of 5.3 percent in 1993, 5.7 percent in 1994, and 5.8 percent in 1995.[7]

The economy began to unravel in the mid-1990s as the result of a complex political crisis, the fall of coffee prices on the world market, and a contraction in the construction sector. The privatization process begun under Gaviria stagnated. The decertification of Colombia by the United States added another element of uncertainty to the Colombian political environment (see Chapter Two). The U.S. sanctions did not succeed in driving President Samper from office, but they reduced business confidence and contributed to the sharpening of the economic crisis.

Colombia's recession deepened as the economy contracted at an annual rate of 7.6 percent in the second quarter of 1999. Urban unem-

---

[6]Jorge Luis Garay S. et al., *Colombia: estructura industrial e internacionalización, 1967–1996*, Tomo I, República de Colombia, Departamento Nacional de Planeación, Bogotá, 1998, pp. 18–22,

[7]Garay, pp. 23–26; KPMG, "Performance of the Economy," www.kpmg.com/co/colombia/performa.htm. Protection against imports raises the cost of producing exports and therefore constitutes an obstacle to the growth of the export sector.

ployment hovered near 20 percent and the government projected a 3.5 percent decline in GDP for the year.[8] The ongoing political violence entailed substantial economic costs. The economic cost of the violence in Colombia has been estimated at between 4 and 9 percent of GDP.[9] The Pastrana government negotiated a $2.7 billion extended fund facility arrangement with the IMF. President Pastrana visited Washington in September 1999 and again in January and April 2000 seeking support for his government's "Plan Colombia" and economic stabilization program.[10] As Colombian economists have noted, political stability is a key condition for the long-term success of any economic stabilization plan.[11] Therefore, whether the economy can be turned around without a reduction in the level of political instability and violence is questionable.

SOCIAL TRENDS

The violence has worsened in Colombia, as the insurgent armed struggle has become more entrenched and widespread. The most violent zones of the country are those where two or more of the actors involved in social conflict—guerrillas, drug cartels, and illegal self-defense (paramilitary) groups—are active. The homicide rate rose from 15 to 92 per 100,000 inhabitants between 1974 and 1995. Homicide rates for males aged 14–44 years increased from 29 to 394 per 100,000 between 1980 and 1995, a 1350 percent increase.[12] "Social intolerance" killings—referred to as *limpiezas* or cleansings— have been on the upswing as both guerrillas and paramilitaries seek

---

[8]*Wall Street Journal*, September 23, 1999.

[9]The figures are difficult to aggregate because of the different methodologies and data sources used in different calculations. Granada and Rojas calculated the total costs associated with the guerrilla conflict between 1990 and 1994 at 4 percent of GDP (in World Bank, "Violence in Colombia: Building Sustainable Peace and Social Capital," Washington, D.C., 2000, Table 2). A report from the Colombian Department of Planning, cited in *Venezuela Analítica*, September 9, 1999, gives the figure as 9 percent of GDP.

[10]See Colombia, Republic of, *Plan Colombia: Plan for Peace, Prosperity, and the Strengthening of the State*, Bogotá, 1999.

[11]Garay, p. 24

[12] World Bank, "Violence in Colombia," pp. 11–12.

to consolidate their control by killing people considered misfits or suspected of collaborating with the other side.[13]

In rural areas, where men and sometimes children join (or are forced to join) guerrilla or paramilitary groups, families and other basic societal units are seriously disrupted. People fleeing violence have been displaced throughout the country, but the levels are highest in the zones with the highest levels of conflict, such as Urabá, the middle Magdalena valley, and the Ariari district. An estimated 35 percent of displacement was reportedly caused by illegal self-defense organizations, 17 percent by the security forces, 24 percent by armed opposition groups, and 24 percent unidentified.[14] The displaced population, which can be taken as an index of societal disruption, was estimated as high as 1,200,000 in 1998.[15]

Law enforcement and judicial institutions have been singularly ineffective in dealing with the violence. According to data presented in an Inter-American Development Bank (IDB) study, the percentage of homicides investigated by the authorities declined from over 80 percent in 1985 to less than 30 percent in 1995. One reason was overload. The increase in the homicide rate in Colombia over the past two decades placed unbearable strains on a traditionally inefficient justice system. Another reason was the contamination of the justice system by violence and intimidation. According to a survey, over 25 percent of the members of the judicial branch had reported threats to themselves or their families.[16]

---

[13]"Gun Law Without Mercy in Colombia's Barrios," *Financial Times*, September 2, 1999.

[14]Amnesty International, 1997 *Annual Report*.

[15]World Bank, "Violence in Colombia," p. 14. The United Nations High Commissioner on Refugees (UNHCR) estimates of the number of displaced persons in Colombia range between 450,000 and 1.6 million spread throughout the country (figures differ depending on the methodology, time frame, and criteria used). The UNHCR notes that though figures vary, studies do agree that displacement is both nationwide and on the increase. See www.unhcr.ch/world/amer/colombia.htm. It is worth noting that this number is about 3 percent of Colombia's population of 40 million. The equivalent number in the United States would be 7.5 million.

[16]See Mauricio Rubio, "La violencia en Colombia: dimensionamiento y políticas de control," Serie de documentos de trabajo R-345, Inter-American Development Bank, Washington, D.C., October 1998, pp. 42–49.

As a World Bank study has noted, the violence has reduced the country's social capital by eroding the effectiveness of judicial, health, educational, media, and security institutions. Death threats, kidnappings, and assassinations have created a well-founded climate of fear. Violence or the threat of violence is meant to influence the administration of justice, the legislative process, and the behavior of the communications media.[17]

The weakness of state and social institutions and the escalating violence and criminal activity have produced a climate of insecurity at all levels of Colombian society and fostered the accelerated growth of privatized armed security groups (see Chapter Five). According to a survey conducted by the Medellín regional authorities, every one of the city's barrios has illegal armed groups that engage in activities ranging from neighborhood vigilance to *limpiezas* and executions of suspected criminals. What these groups appear to have in common is a complete lack of confidence in the state and its security and judicial institutions.[18]

Although the incentives for the growth of these "private justice" groups are strong in light of the state's inability to provide security to local communities, the existence of these groups is itself a factor of violence that contributes to the atomization of society and the growing chaos in Colombia. The socially destructive aspect of this phenomenon is amplified when these groups develop links to organized criminal networks.

ROADMAP TO THE REPORT

The synergy of which this report speaks has deep roots. Chapter Two discusses the scope and dimensions of the drug trade in Colombia and its impact on Colombia, the region, and U.S. interests, and concludes with an assessment of the U.S. response. The next three chapters deal with the alternative armed power centers—what the Colombians call "agents of violence." Chapters Three and Four describe the origin and development of the major guerrilla groups—the Revolutionary Armed Forces of Colombia (FARC) and the National

---

[17]World Bank, "Violence in Colombia," pp. 24–25.

[18]Rubio, p. 28, fn. 109.

Liberation Army (ELN)—their links to the drug trade and arms trafficking networks, and their political objectives and strategy. Chapter Five deals with one of the least understood but increasingly important factors in the Colombian conflict, the illegal self-defense forces, or paramilitaries, as they are commonly called.

The following three chapters analyze the Colombian government response to the forces challenging its authority. Chapter Six provides an assessment of Plan Colombia, the centerpiece of the Colombian government's approach, its focus on the counter-narcotics component, and the U.S. government's supporting role. Chapter Seven discusses the peace negotiations between the government and the guerrillas and the prospects for a peace settlement. Chapter Eight outlines possible alternative scenarios for Colombia, ranging from a successful peace agreement or the strengthening of the government to continued deterioration or collapse and offers a best estimate of what Colombia's future path might be. Chapter Nine, "A Wider Conflict?," notes that the contraction of the Colombian government's authority has already facilitated the spread of guerrilla activity and drug trafficking to neighboring states and discusses the regional implications of a widening of the conflict. Drawing on the analysis of the preceding chapters, Chapter Ten discusses the implications of the above for U.S. interests. The appendix assesses the Colombian armed forces, including the ongoing effort at military reform and the armed forces' posture, mobility, patterns of recruitment, and budget.

Chapter Two

THE ILLEGAL DRUG TRADE

SCOPE AND DIMENSIONS

Colombia is currently the world's principal producer and distributor of refined cocaine, the vast majority of which (70 percent) is exported to the U.S. market. In 1999, the country refined approximately 520 metric tons of cocaine, representing roughly 80 percent of global production.[1] The narcotic is typically produced in a three-stage process. Coca leaves are first crushed and boiled with limewater and kerosene to produce coca paste. This is then mixed with sulphuric acid, potassium permanganate (sulphur dioxide can also be used), and ammonium hydroxide, filtered, and dried into a cocaine base. The amalgam is finally dissolved in acetone to form a white precipitate of cocaine hydrochloride (CHCl), which is trapped (generally by straining), dried, and pressed into bricks for shipping.[2] The refined

---

[1]U.S. Department of State, Bureau for International Narcotics and Law Enforcement Affairs, *International Narcotics Control Strategy Report, 1999*, Washington, D.C.: 2000. The figures put out by the U.S. State Department are generally recognized as the most comprehensive and accurate available. It needs to be noted, however, that the figures used in the data are theoretical, representing estimates of total potential production on the assumption that all available crops are converted into finished drugs. Since these approximations do not make allowance for losses resulting from refining inefficiency, bad weather, disease, or interdiction, real totals are almost certainly lower than the figures in the State Department's annual report. Nonetheless, they serve as useful mean reference points in a given statistical range.

[2]"Crack" is a derivative of cocaine that began to appear in the 1990s. It is made by mixing CHCl with baking powder, soda, and water to form a cake that is then cooked until a hard substance is formed. This is then broken down ("cracked") to reveal crystals of pure cocaine hydrochloride that are processed into small crystals about the size

narcotic is usually snorted through the nasal passages, although it can also be injected intravenously.[3]

Traditionally, most of the primary base used for Colombian cocaine production was imported from Peru and Bolivia. However, this has changed over the last few years—largely as a result of the U.S. "air-bridge" strategy (see The U.S. Response, below)—with Colombia now primarily responsible for all stages of the cocaine production process, including initial harvesting. Reflecting this, by 1999 the country had registered a net increase of over 28 percent in its overall coca cultivation to 122,500 hectares, continuing a trend that started in 1997.[4] U.S. Department of Justice officials expected this base to translate into a 50 percent increase in overall refined cocaine exports during 2000.[5]

In addition to cocaine, Colombia is the Western Hemisphere's largest producer and distributor of refined heroin.[6] This narcotic is synthe-sized by boiling morphine base (itself a derivative of the dried, chemically altered sap of the opium poppy)[7] with acetic anhydride.

---

of raisins, which are then smoked (known as "freebasing"). The psychotropic and physiological effects of cocaine and crack cocaine are the same, but the intensity and duration of each can differ. Crack always gives a fast, intense high, sometimes lasting only a few minutes. Cocaine, when taken intravenously, gives an intense high similar to that of crack. When it is snorted, the high is less intense, though of longer duration.

[3]"Cocaine Production, Manufacturing Methods, Equipment Used, Chemicals Needed. Drug Information for DARE Officers, Parents, Teachers, Students and Researchers," http://www.mninter.net/~publish/COKE/index2.htm.

[4]U.S. Department of State, *International Narcotics Control Strategy Report, 1999*. See also, "Lack of Air Support Hindering Drug War," *Washington Post*, March 3, 2000; "A Muddle in the Jungle," *The Economist*, March 4, 2000; "DEA: Colombian Cocaine Production Up," *CNN Interactive World Wide News*, January 18, 2000. It should be noted that coca production in Peru has once again started to rise.

[5]Testimony by William Ledwith, Chief of the U.S. Drug Enforcement Agency's International Operations, before the House Government Reform Committee, Criminal Justice, Drug Policy and Human Resources Subcommittee, Washington, D.C., February 15, 2000.

[6]In global terms, however, less than 2 percent of the world's opium and refined heroin comes from Colombia, with most production taking place either in the "Golden Triangle" of Southeast Asia or the "Golden Crescent" of Southwest Asia.

[7]Opium gum is produced by mixing and boiling the sap of the opium poppy in lime water. The resulting white precipitate is drawn off, reheated with ammonia, filtered, and boiled again until it is reduced into a brown paste. This is finally dried in the sun to form morphine base.

Sodium carbonate is then added to the mixture, causing an amalgam to collect and solidify. The mixture is collected and purified with ether and hydrochloric acid to form standardized Number 4 heroin, which, because it is water soluble, tends to be taken intravenously.[8] In 1999, U.S. State Department estimates showed Colombian poppy cultivation to be 7500 hectares, a crop capable of producing roughly eight tons of refined heroin.[9] As with cocaine, the main target for the bulk of this opium derivative is the United States, currently accounting for 65 percent of all shipments that are exported from Colombia.[10]

Traffickers use several methods and routes to export cocaine and heroin to the United States, which remains the largest and most reliable market for the Colombian narcotics trade. A large percentage of the shipments is trafficked through Central America (primarily Costa Rica, Honduras, Nicaragua, and El Salvador) or flown up the central Pacific coast to Mexico, which acts as the main gateway for the North American market.[11] Most consignments are then moved into the United States by syndicates based in the Tijuana, Gulf of Mexico, and Ciudad Juarez border regions, many of which have gained a reputation for smuggling expertise after years of running illegal alien operations into Texas and California.[12]

A second passage runs northeast to Florida, either directly or via Haiti, the Dominican Republic, Puerto Rico, or the Lesser Antilles. This route was used extensively during the early 1990s, but was then by-passed in favor of the Mexican conduit after successful interdiction operations in the Eastern Caribbean. In the last two years, how-

---

[8]Frontline, "The Opium Kings: Transforming Opium Poppies into Heroin," http://www.pbs.org/wgbh/pages/frontline/shows/heroin/transform/ (no date available).

[9]U.S. Department of State, *International Narcotics Control Strategy Report, 1999.*

[10]Ledwith testimony; "Colombia Seizes 30 Percent More Cocaine, Heroin in 1998," *CNN Interactive World Wide News*, December 19, 1999; "Clinton Plans to Seek US$1.3 Billion to Stem Colombian Drug Flow," *Washington Post*, January 12, 2000.

[11]Up to 70 percent of illicit drugs that enter the United States are smuggled through Mexico.

[12]International Institute of Strategic Studies, "International Drug Trade," *Strategic Survey*, 1997/98, Oxford University Press, London, 1998, p. 249; "Major Suspect in Drug Trafficking Arrested in Mexico," *CNN Interactive World Wide News*, March 12, 2000; "Drugs Flood in from Mexico," *Washington Post*, November 29, 1999.

ever, there once again appears to have been a return to the Caribbean passage as a result of heightened Mexican counternarcotics efforts. This ability to adapt to changing threats and opportunities reflects the inherently dynamic and "hydra-like" quality of the contemporary Colombian drug trade.[13] In recent years, West Africa has also emerged as an increasingly important trafficking transshipment point for the United States as well as for Europe and secondary destinations in South Africa (particularly Cape Town, Durban, and Johannesburg).

THE MAIN PLAYERS

Prior to 1994, the Cali and Medellín cartels dominated virtually all aspects of the Colombian drug business, which then focused more or less exclusively on cocaine. However, since the death of Medellín kingpin Pablo Escobar in 1993, as well as the capture of leading members of the Cali inner circle, control of the country's drug trade has become dispersed. Newer, less-structured, and "flatter" organizations now appear to be in the ascendancy, most of which operate in small, autonomous cells that are linked via Internet chat rooms and cellular phones protected by the very latest in encryption technology.[14] Unlike the previous cartels, these "boutique" groups typically contract out the majority of their jobs to specialists who work on a job-to-job basis rather than as part of an integrated structure.[15]

The new syndicates have also increasingly diversified their operations into opiates, reacting to growing consumer demand in the

---

[13]Discussion with Dr. Bruce Bagley, University of Miami, February 11, 2000. See also Ledwith testimony; Peter Zirnite, "The Militarization of the Drug War in Latin America," *Current History*, 97/618, 1998, p. 169; Phil Williams, "The Nature of Drug-Trafficking Networks," *Current History*, 97/618, 1998, p. 157; "Drugs Flood in from Mexico," *Washington Post*, November 29, 1999.

[14]This is very much reflective of the general "network" organizational paradigm that has been developed by John Arquilla and David Ronfeldt. See John Arquilla and David Ronfeldt, *The Advent of Netwar*, RAND, MR-789, 1996.

[15]Discussion at USSOUTHCOM, Miami, February 10, 2000. See also Ledwith testimony; Peter Chalk, "Heroin and Cocaine: A Global Threat," *Janes' Intelligence Review*, p. 11; Geopolitical Drug Watch, "A Drug Primer for the Late 1990s," *Current History*, 97/618, 1998, pp. 150–151; "New Cartels Hold Tech Advantage," *Washington Post*, November 15, 1999.

United States for higher-grade heroin that need not be injected intravenously. By offering the drug at a lower price than traditional Southeast Asian suppliers, the Colombians have successfully managed to capture much of the lucrative U.S. heroin market, as well as cater to a growing generation of poly-drug users who take opiates to cushion the severe crash that typically follows a cocaine high.[16]

U.S. authorities admit that they have only limited operational intelligence on the groups that now dominate the drug trade in Colombia, attributing this to the groups' less-structured nature. Of most concern is the fact that these transient syndicates necessarily lack the operational "footprints" of more established organizations, which has made it far harder for law enforcement authorities to build an accurate picture of dimensions, intentions, and capabilities. The irony is that changes in this direction have largely been driven by law enforcement successes against the larger and more visible Cali and Medellín cartels. As the Paris-based Geopolitical Drug Watch Group observes: "The immediate effect of [past] repression was to disorganize the networks. But by making a virtue out of necessity, these large organizations quickly realized that decentralized structures are much less vulnerable and began the process of transforming themselves accordingly."[17]

The clearest window into the changes surrounding Colombian drug structures came in late 1999 when Operation *Millennium*, a joint U.S.-Colombian venture, successfully disrupted the activities of the Alejandro Bernal group. During the course of 1999, the DEA estimated the syndicate had been responsible for shipping 20 to 30 metric tons of cocaine every month to the United States, working in conjunction with the Mexican Ciudad Juarez-based cartel. Following the operation, however, U.S. and Colombian intelligence sources conceded that the Bernal group did not appear to be a single entity but rather an amorphous organization into which several other

---

[16]U.S. Department of State, *International Narcotics Control Strategy Report, 1999*; Australian Bureau of Criminal Intelligence, *Australian Illicit Drug Report 1997–98*, Canberra, 1998, p. 34.

[17]Geopolitical Drug Watch, p. 151.

smaller cells fed and contracted, sometimes for single, one-off operations.[18]

This ad hoc, disaggregated quality of the contemporary Colombian drug trade effectively means that the arrest of Bernal and his associates[19] will not have much impact on the overall flow of cocaine into the United States. As one Colombian counter-narcotics official conceded at the conclusion of *Millennium*: Following the arrest of Bernal,

> we [now] estimate there are several hundred small cartels operating in an atomized fashion. Several of those groups fed into the organization we dismantled. But there are several other people out there as big as Bernal, who can put loads together from small organizations, and we don't even have them identified.[20]

As discussed in greater detail in the following chapter, the country's major guerrilla organization, the Revolutionary Armed Forces of Colombia (FARC); right-wing paramilitary organizations; and, to a lesser extent, elements of the National Liberation Army (ELN) also play important roles in the Colombian drug trade.

IMPACT OF DRUG TRADE ON COLOMBIA AND THE REGION

The cocaine trade has brought about what some have called a "demographic revolution" in Colombia. Economic opportunities created by production, processing, and marketing of coca products attracted large numbers of migrants to the coca-growing areas of southeastern Colombia. In the Caguán area, in the southern FARC-controlled "demilitarized zone," the drug trade has attracted a large floating population, many of whom accept FARC guerrillas as the

---

[18]Ledwith testimony; see also "Drug Cartels Hold Tech Advantage," *Washington Post*, November 15, 1999; "Major Arrests Sabotage Colombian Drug Network," *Washington Post*, October 14, 1999.

[19]The operation also resulted in the indictment of Fabio Ochoa-Vasquez, one of the former leaders of the Medellín cartel, along with 30 other defendants.

[20]Quoted in "Drug Cartels Hold Tech Advantage," *Washington Post*, November 15, 1999.

main guardians of their newfound "narco-economy."[21] This development has expanded the social base of the guerrillas and complicated counter-narcotics efforts in the area.

The heroin and cocaine trade has fueled high rates of drug-related crime and violence. During the 1990s, the country was repeatedly wracked by bomb attacks, kidnappings, and shootings designed to intimidate government officials and coerce changes in policy, particularly with regard to extradition of suspected Colombian drug traffickers to the United States.

Interfactional fighting, both within and between cartels, has also been a common feature, reaching a zenith in 1993 when a virtual civil war broke out between Pablo Escobar and a rival vigilante group, *los pepes*. Overall, it is estimated that drug-related violence currently accounts for a high proportion of the country's 30,000 annual murders, one of the highest homicide rates of any country outside a war zone and more than double the number of murders recorded in the United States during 1998.[22]

Politically, the impact has been rampant corruption, undermining both governmental legitimacy and executive authority. Heroin and cocaine remain the most lucrative commodities on the black market. Estimates of the valuation of the illegal drugs sold in the United States vary widely. By one gauge, the 520 metric tons of cocaine that Colombia produced in 1999 could, at an average retail street price in the United States of one hundred dollars a gram (or $100 million per metric ton), have netted as much as $52 billion—more than the gross domestic product of many nations. Even if only a fraction of these revenues returns directly to the drug syndicates as profits, overall earnings would remain in the hundreds of millions, if not billions of dollars.[23]

---

[21]Camilo Echandía Castilla, *El Conflicto Armado y las Manifestaciones de la Violencia en las Regiones de Colombia*, Presidencia de la República de Colombia, Oficina del Alto Comisionado para la Paz, Bogotá, 2000, p. 79.

[22]See figures in the *Federal Bureau of Investigation (FBI) Supplementary Homicide Reports, 1976–1998*, http://www.oip.usdoj.gov/bjs/homicide/city.htm.

[23]U.S. Department of State, *International Narcotics Control Strategy Report, 1999*.

Revenues of this magnitude have given the various syndicates involved in the Colombian drug trade a virtually open-ended capacity to corrupt.[24] This was perhaps best reflected by the enormous loss of international and domestic legitimacy that befell the Colombian government after it became apparent that drug syndicates had helped finance the 1994 election campaign of President Ernesto Samper.[25]

The drug trade has also affected wider Andean stability. Colombian cartels and narco-insurgents now routinely cross over into the adjacent territories of Panama, Venezuela, Brazil, Ecuador, and Peru, exploiting poorly monitored border regions for safe havens as well as to facilitate the regional movement of drugs. Narcotics have played their part in helping to stimulate a growing cross-frontier migration and refugee problem. The Colombian government's inability to secure its borders has severely complicated Bogotá's regional relations, particularly with Venezuela, Ecuador, and Panama.[26]

IMPACT OF THE DRUG TRADE ON U.S. INTERESTS

While these invasive socio-political effects have generated growing concern in Washington, it is the consequences of the Colombian drug trade on the United States itself that are stimulating most American interest. Crack and cocaine sales drive much of the coun-

---

[24]See, for instance, United States Commission on National Security/21st Century, *New World Coming: American Security in the 21st Century*, Phase I Report on the Emerging Global Security Environment for the First Quarter of the 21st Century, September 15, 1999, p. 108.

[25]Arlene Tickner, "Colombia: Chronicle of a Crisis Foretold," *Current History*, 97/616, 1998, p. 64; *Europa World Year Book*, "Colombia," Europa Publications, London, 1999, pp. 1006–1007. In January 1996, former defense minister Fernando Botero testified that Samper was aware his campaign had been financed by contributions of approximately US$6 million from drug traffickers. Following the revelations, the United States began to identify Colombia's drug problem directly with President Samper and work toward his departure from power.

[26]Gabriel Marcella and Donald Schulz, "Colombia's Three Wars: U.S. Strategy at the Crossroads," SSI, U.S. Army War College, Carlisle Barracks, March 5, 1999, pp. 13–16; Bruce M. Bagley, "The Evolution of Drug Trafficking in Colombia in the 1990s," unpublished paper provided to authors, February 2000, pp. 12–13; Michael Shifter, "The United States and Colombia: Partners in Ambiguity," *Current History*, 99/634, 2000, p. 53; and "Civil War Displaces 1 Million Colombians in Five Years," *CNN Interactive World Wide News*, February 22, 2000.

try's drug-related violence as rival gangs compete for lucrative sales territory and addicts steal to feed their habit. Major metropolitan centers such as Los Angeles, New York, Chicago, Washington, and Miami have been especially hard hit, where drugs have played an important role in accelerating already serious levels of social decline and inner-city decay.[27]

Heroin and cocaine have also had a serious health impact in the United States. Although cocaine and crack use gradually declined during the 1990s, some 5.7 million Americans were estimated to be taking the drug in 1999 (compared to 7.7 million in 1990 and 6.6 million in 1995). In the same time frame, there has been a rising trend in the use of heroin, which has witnessed a 15 percent increase in demand since 1990. More problematic, there has been an escalation in multiple-drug use, with law enforcement authorities increasingly reporting seizures of packs containing both heroin and cocaine (commonly known as speedballs). The consequences of this combined substance abuse have been severe, contributing to a surge in emergency room admissions.[28]

During the 1990s—a decade in which Colombia emerged as the main source for the two drugs in the United States—Washington spent an average of $57.7 billion every year on law enforcement, interdiction, educational, rehabilitation, and health-related programs designed to stem the flow of heroin and cocaine and manage their effects. The budget for international drug control operations in FY2000 amounted to approximately one and a half billion dollars. If one were to add indirect losses brought about by the use of these narcotics, including curtailed job opportunities and decreased workplace productivity, overall economic costs would be far higher. As the Office of National Drug Control Policy observes, this financial burden is shared by all of society, either directly or indirectly through higher tax dollars.[29]

---

[27]U.S. Department of State, *International Narcotics Control Strategy Report, 1999.*

[28]Total hospital cocaine-related admissions, for instance, rose from 80,355 in 1990 to 172,014 in 1998, while those associated with heroin more than doubled from 33,884 to 77,645 during the same period. Office of National Drug Control Policy, National Control Strategy, 2000, http://www.whitehousedrugpolicy.gov, March 1, 2000.

[29]Ibid.

THE U.S. RESPONSE

Since 1993, U.S. external counter-narcotics interdiction efforts have essentially concentrated on tackling the problem at its source, in Colombia. Prior to this, most of Washington's initiatives had been directed toward stopping cocaine as it moved through the Mexican and Caribbean transit states. The shift in focus, which was formalized in Presidential Decision Directive (PDD) 14, was precipitated by the reasoning that since no other alternative existed for production and refining, this represented the weakest link in the overall cocaine industry chain.[30]

Between 1994 and 1999, efforts were aimed at augmenting the counter-narcotics capabilities of the Colombian National Police in addition to attacking the so-called air-bridge that connects crop growers in Bolivia and Peru with refiners in Colombia. Two rationales underscored the twin approach. First, better law enforcement training, aimed at sound investigative techniques and criminal prosecutions, was seen as the most effective way of countering the drug lords and undermining their operations. Second, it was assumed that if air shipments of coca were disrupted, the overhead costs for the Colombian refiners would rise, generating price increases that would inevitably be passed onto U.S. consumers, thereby reducing the street demand for cocaine.[31] Revelations that the Cali cartel had financed President Ernesto Samper's 1994 presidential election campaign led the Clinton administration to decertify Colombia from U.S. counter-narcotics assistance and aid between 1996 and 1997. However, police and air interdiction support was maintained on the grounds that it was a critical component of wider counter-drug efforts in the Andean region.[32]

---

[30]Zirnite, p. 169.

[31]U.S. Department of State, *International Narcotics Control Strategy Report, 1999.*

[32]In 1986, the U.S. Congress amended the Foreign Assistance Act of 1961 to include a provision that for a major drug-producing and/or transit country to have its counter-narcotics credentials certified, the President must certify that it is actively seeking to control the production/flow of drugs within its borders, either on its own or in conjunction with the United States. In certain cases, a country may be granted certification, notwithstanding its failure to meet this criterion, on the grounds that it is vital for national security interests. This happened with regard to Colombia in 1995, allowing the overall flow of U.S. aid to remain unaltered that year. Between 1996 and 1997, however, the country was fully decertified, which with the exception of counter-

Despite some tactical successes in reducing coca production in Peru and Bolivia, the overall impact of the police/air-bridge strategy has been limited if not counterproductive. If air interdiction has been successful in reducing the number of coca flights from Bolivia and Peru, it has merely prompted Colombian refiners to grow their own base material, causing a major boost in indigenous leaf cultivation. More seriously, the air-bridge strategy has given the drug producers an incentive to diversify into opiates, with syndicates increasingly seeking to offset commodity production disruptions in one area by expanding operations in another. This development has both exacerbated and further complicated the overall Colombian drug problem.[33]

These consequences have caused a shift in U.S. counter-narcotics efforts to an explicit emphasis on support for the military's counter-narcotics operations. The aim, according to official rhetoric, is a "'full court press' on all trafficking organization members and critical nodes to completely disrupt [and] destroy their production and shipping capabilities."[34] The new policy tools emphasized in this absolute "war on drugs" are equipment transfers, crop eradication, and militarized counter-narcotics training—details of which will be discussed in Chapter Six.

The United States has also stressed the necessity of increased crop eradication in its revamped counter-narcotics strategy, to be carried out by the Colombian National Police once crop-growing/refining regions have been secured by the military. Current projections call for 80,000 hectares to be sprayed (largely in Putumayo), which, if achieved, will bring the annual total to roughly 65 percent of the area currently thought to be under cultivation.[35] Fifteen specially de-

---

narcotics support to the National Police, essentially froze all American assistance for the two years.

[33]Discussion with Dr. Bagley; see also Zirnite, p. 170; "A Muddle in the Jungle," *The Economist*, March 4, 2000; and "A New War," *The Economist*, January 15, 2000.

[34]Cited in Zirnite, p. 168. See also Michael Shifter, "Colombia at War," *Current History* 98/626, 1999, pp. 120–121.

[35]29,000 hectares of coca fields were reportedly destroyed from December 2000 to February 2001. *Financial Times*, February 20, 2001. The total area under coca cultivation in Colombia was estimated by the U.S. Department of State at 122,500 hectares in 1999. Other estimates are higher. It is perhaps worth noting that crop fumigation and eradication rarely represent a permanent solution to drug production.

signed fumigation aircraft are due to be transferred to Colombia in 2001, augmenting the eight planes already in action. The Black Hawk and Huey helicopters that have been earmarked for Colombian counter-narcotics duties will provide protection for these aerial herbicidal missions.[36] This counter-narcotics strategy that targets the coca fields in southern Colombia is referred to as the "Southern strategy" or the "Drive to the South."

Crops are either grown in new areas or reseeded in the same plot once soil microbes have decomposed the coca and poppy herbicides—a cycle that typically takes a year to complete. See "We're Targeting a Colombia That We Don't Fully Understand," *Washington Post*, April 2, 2000; "The Andean Coca Wars: A Crop That Refuses to Die," *The Economist*, March 4, 2000; and "Spraying Doesn't Stem Illegal Drug Crops in Colombia," *CNN Interactive World Wide News*, February 21, 2000.

[36] Bagley, "The Evolution of Drug Trafficking in Colombia in the 1990s," p. 16; U.S. Department of State, *International Narcotics Control Strategy Report, 1999;* "A Muddle in the Jungle," *The Economist*, March 4, 2000; "The Andean Coca Wars: A Crop That Refuses to Die," *The Economist*, March 4, 2000; "Spraying Doesn't Stem Illegal Drug Crops in Colombia," *CNN Interactive World Wide News*, February 21, 2000; "Colombia Expects Peasants to Fight Cocaine Removal," *CNN Interactive World Wide News*, February 4, 2000.

Chapter Three

ORIGINS AND DEVELOPMENT OF THE GUERRILLAS

Colombia's physical and socio-political landscape—a territory fragmented by mountain ranges and tropical forests, deficient infrastructure, lack of national integration, and the tradition of armed revolts against the central authorities—has provided fertile ground for guerrillas. Guerrilla warfare shading into politicized banditry has been, in fact, the most prevalent form of armed activity in the country's civil conflicts since colonial times.

The patterns of Colombia's current armed conflict were set in the period of widespread political violence appropriately known as *la violencia*. *La violencia* began after the assassination of Liberal Party leader Jorge Eliécer Gaitán on April 9, 1948, and intensified after a Conservative victory in 1949, in an election that the Liberal Party boycotted. In the years that followed, the Liberal and Conservative parties mobilized armed supporters in the countryside in an undeclared civil war that claimed over 200,000 lives.

THE REVOLUTIONARY ARMED FORCES OF COLOMBIA (FARC)

The major guerrilla organization, the Revolutionary Armed Forces of Colombia (FARC), is part of this tradition. The FARC leader, Manuel Marulanda Vélez, better known as Tirofijo ("Sureshot"), began his guerrilla career in 1949 when he joined a Liberal guerrilla band in the department of Tolima, an epicenter of the violence.[1] In 1964, Maru-

---

[1] Marulanda was born Pedro Antonio Marín in Quindío in 1930; he changed his name to Manuel Marulanda in honor of a union leader of the same name killed by the security forces. See "El viejo guerrillero y su delfín," *El Mundo* (Madrid), July 11, 1998.

landa helped to establish a Communist-oriented "independent republic" in Marquetalia, a remote area in southern Tolima. It was one of several "republics" established by Communist-oriented guerrillas in southern Colombia.[2] Marulanda escaped when the Colombian army attacked and destroyed the Marquetalia guerrilla group in June 1964. In 1966, the Communist guerrillas, denominated "Communist self-defense forces," were reorganized as the Revolutionary Armed Forces of Colombia (FARC), with Marulanda as Chief of Staff.

The FARC expanded slowly between the mid-1960s and the 1980s. In its early stages, FARC guerrillas engaged in ambushes of military units and raids on farms. The main objectives were capturing military equipment, securing food and supplies, capturing hostages, and settling scores with informers. Those activities were restricted to the areas where the guerrillas had historically operated. Far from attacking the "nerve centers of the country," as the FARC manifesto of May 1966 asserted, the FARC was more concerned with survival in the face of a determined effort by the Colombian army to eliminate it. In this formative period, the FARC began to take on the accoutrements of an army by wearing uniforms and insignia and establishing a code with severe punishments for banditry, crimes of passion, and informing.[3]

In 1969, the FARC opened a second guerrilla front in the middle Magdalena valley, in an inhospitable but strategic area on the border between the departments of Boyacá and Santander. In 1971, it established a third front in the Urabá area, in the Darien gap between Panama and Colombia. In 1974, the organization established a general staff and a secretariat to provide political direction. In the 1980s, the FARC began to implement the expansion strategy set at its 1982 Seventh Conference. Each existing front was to grow another front,

---

[2]Others were established in Rio Chiquito, El Pato-Guayabero, and Santa Barbara. They were eradicated by the Colombian army in counter-insurgency campaigns from 1963 to 1966.

[3]Richard Maullin, *Soldiers, Guerrillas, and Politics in Colombia*, RAND, R-0630-ARPA, 1971, pp. 28–41.

until there was at least one for each of Colombia's fifty-odd departments.[4]

A front is not a military unit of any particular size; it refers to a guerrilla command operating in a geographic jurisdiction. Within the
front jurisdiction there are combat, support, and infrastructure elements. Usually the core of the front is the combat units, generally
one or several companies. A column consists of two or more companies. A company consists of some 50–55 fighters, divided into two
platoons called guerrillas, each consisting of approximately 25 fighters. Platoons are further subdivided into squads of seven or eight
fighters. Besides the combat units there are commissions, staffed by
militia members. The finance commission is in charge of collecting
"taxes." In addition, there are logistics commissions, intelligence
commissions, public order commissions, mass work commissions,
and others as may be designated by the front commander.[5]

The FARC grew in the 1980s by tapping into revenues obtained by
exploiting primary commodities—a phenomenon identified in recent World Bank studies to explain the growth of rebel movements in
several developing countries.[6] The FARC took advantage of a cease-
fire with the government of President Belisario Betancur from 1984
to 1987 to expand and consolidate its operations in resource-rich
areas (cattle in the eastern plains, commercial agriculture in Urabá
and Santander, oil in the middle Magdalena valley, and gold in
Antioquia). Three new fronts were established in Caquetá and Meta,
the departments east of the easternmost range of the Andes, which
are now the source of much of Colombia's coca crop, and two more

---

[4]Departments are the political divisions into which the country is divided (there is also
a Special District covering the capital, Bogotá). Departments are divided in turn into
municipios (urban areas) and *corregimientos* (rural areas).

[5]We are indebted to this discussion of FARC front organization to David Spencer, an
expert on guerrilla warfare and Colombian military issues and one of the reviewers of
this report.

[6]This line of analysis has been developed most fully in research sponsored by the
World Bank on civil conflicts, crime, and violence. See Paul Collier and Anke Hoeffler,
"Justice-Seeking and Loot-Seeking in Civil War," World Bank 1999.

were established in the middle Magdalena valley.[7] The FARC also derived income from smuggling in the border regions.[8]

At this time the FARC began to develop linkages with the illegal drug industry, whose production facilities were located largely in the areas into which the guerrillas were expanding their operations. How this linkage came about may have a bearing on the dynamics of the current triangular government-guerrilla-paramilitary struggle. The policy of taxing the drug industry and mobilizing and recruiting people in the lower end of the drug business was laid out formally in the unpublished "Conclusions" of the FARC Seventh Conference.[9] According to a political leader in Guaviare, until 1981 the insurgents in that area forbade the cultivation of coca and marijuana, which they considered counter-revolutionary. At that time drug traffickers, protected by paramilitaries, began to move into the region, and coca cultivation developed into the dominant economic activity. Fearing the loss of their social base—agricultural migrants—to their political enemies, the guerrillas began to promote and protect the coca crop themselves.[10]

In the 1990s, FARC fronts proliferated in the coca-growing regions east of the Andes—nine new fronts were active in the department of Meta alone. New fronts were also established closer to the country's population centers and economically strategic regions, including five new fronts in Cundinamarca, the department closest to the capital, Bogotá.

The FARC grew from 350 fighters at its founding in 1966 to approximately 3600 in 32 fronts in 1986, 7000 in 60 fronts in 1995, and

---

[7]Camilo Echandía Castilla, pp. 45–47.

[8]Ibid., p. 47.

[9]Personal communication from David Spencer, December 2000.

[10]Presentation by José Olarte (mayor of Calamar, Guaviare), at Georgetown University and National Endowment for Democracy Conference on "Local Government Amidst the Armed Conflict: The Experience of Colombian Mayors," Georgetown University, Washington, D.C., September 27, 2000. The same dynamic might be at work in the former ELN strongholds in southern Bolívar, where paramilitaries have succeeded in capturing part of the ELN's social base by extending and protecting the coca economy.

15,000–20,000 in over 70 fronts in 2000.[11]   The long-term goal was
the creation of a force of 30,000, which in the FARC's estimation
would enable the organization to engage in large-scale offensive operations against the main units of the Colombian army.[12]

The FARC is organized into seven territorial "blocs," each composed
of four to five fronts in the smaller blocs to 15 to 20 in the larger ones
(see Figure 3.1). Each front in turn is composed of columns of up to a
hundred fighters. The seven FARC blocs are

1. The eastern bloc, with 21 fronts, covers the region east of the eastern cordillera of the Andes and the central departments of Cundinamarca and Boyacá. Its strategic task is to cut off the populous
   central highlands from the eastern plains and the Amazonian region.

2. The northwestern bloc, with eight fronts, operates in the departments of Antioquia, Chocó, and Córdoba. This bloc controls a
   corridor from the Panamanian border and the adjacent Atlantic
   and Pacific coasts to the middle Magdalena valley.

3. The middle Magdalena bloc is active in the area of the same
   name. Its units operate in parts of the departments of Antioquia,
   Bolívar, Cesar, Santander, and Boyacá.

4. The southern bloc covers the FARC's strongholds in southern
   Colombia, in the departments of Caquetá, Huila, Putumayo, and
   part of Cauca. This area also includes most of the "demilitarized
   zone" conceded to the FARC by the Colombian government.

5. The western (or southwestern) bloc operates in the departments
   of Nariño, Cauca, and Valle, the region from the western cordillera
   of the Andes to the Pacific Ocean and down to the Ecuadorean
   border.

---

[11]Alfredo Rangel Suárez, *Colombia: guerra en el fin de siglo,* Tercer Mundo Editores,
Bogotá, 1998, p. 12. Estimates of the number of FARC fronts and urban organizations
vary.

[12]Karl Penhaul, "Colombian Rebels Map Out Plan to Topple Government," News
Agency Colombia, January 14, 1999. David Spencer, *FARC Warfare Strategy and Tactics 1996–1999,* unpublished manuscript.

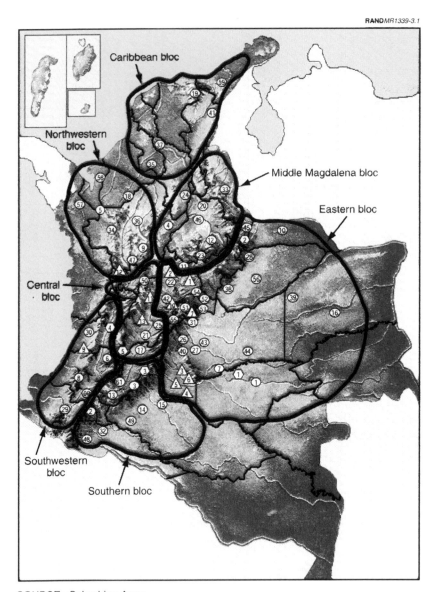

RAND*MR1339-3.1*

SOURCE: Colombian Army.

Figure 3.1—Location of FARC Blocs and Fronts

6. The central bloc, with four fronts, is not as active as the others; it operates in the strategic central region of Colombia, where the land lines of communication between Medellín, Cali, and Bogotá converge.

7. The northern (or Caribbean) bloc, which also has registered a relatively low level of activity, operates in the Atlantic coast departments and on the Venezuelan border.[13]

In addition, there are 15 independent companies (equivalent to fronts) assigned to the different blocs and used as a reserve by the bloc commander. There are also mobile columns under the direct control of the FARC secretariat. These independent companies and mobile columns are given names (usually of historical figures or revolutionary heroes) rather than numbers.[14]

Despite the FARC's ability to expand its military forces and the areas where they operate, the organization has some critical weaknesses, notably its linkage to criminal elements and its lack of support among the population at large. Opinion polls estimate overall FARC support at about 5 percent of the population. Although the FARC has some support in the urban areas, its presence in the cities is limited.[15] In the areas where it predominates, the FARC has endeavored to institutionalize popular support by setting up political support groups, but in fact it enforces its rule largely through selective terror and intimidation. That said, the Bogotá authorities have not been successful in turning the lack of popular support for the guerrillas into active support for the government.[16] Local opposition to the guerrillas has developed spontaneously, largely outside of government control, in the form of the illegal self-defense forces, commonly known as paramilitaries.

---

[13]Echandía, pp. 49–50.

[14]Spencer, "FARC Warfare Strategy and Tactics," pp. 23–24.

[15]David Spencer and Heather Noss, *Colombia: Strategic End State, Goals, and Means: A Workshop Report,* Center for Strategic Studies, The CNA Corporation, Arlington, Virginia, November 2000, p. 5.

[16]David Passage stresses the importance of active popular support for the success of any government's efforts to defeat guerrilla movements. David Passage, "Colombia's Struggle," *Adelante,* Summer 2000, pp. 19–20.

THE NATIONAL LIBERATION ARMY (ELN)

Adherents of Cuban-style revolution founded the National Liberation Army (ELN) in 1964. Unlike the FARC's peasant-origin leadership, the ELN leadership was composed of students and graduates of the University of Santander. At a time of tension between Havana and Moscow over revolutionary strategy in Latin America, the ELN came to be the Colombian guerrilla movement favored by Havana, whereas the FARC was aligned with the Soviets and the Moscow-line Colombian Communist Party.

Aside from its Castroite component, the ELN attracted radicalized Catholics who blended Catholic teachings of social justice with Marxist ideology. The most notable of these recruits was Father Camilo Torres, a Louvain-educated Catholic priest from a socially prominent Colombian family, who joined the ELN in October 1965 and was killed in an encounter with the army four months later.

Like the FARC, the ELN initially operated in a restricted geographical setting—the northern departments of Santander, Antioquia, and Bolívar—which the ELN sought to turn into a Colombian version of the Sierra Maestra, Fidel Castro's mountain stronghold in Cuba. As a military organization, the ELN failed to mount operations of any consequence, partly because of lack of support by the local population and partly because of ideological rifts within the organization. Several commanders opposed to ELN leader Fabio Vásquez Castaño were convicted of treason by revolutionary tribunals and executed, while others escaped death by surrendering to the Colombian army. Information provided by these deserters enabled the army to kill or capture most of the ELN active membership by the end of the 1960s.[17]

The ELN reemerged in the 1980s under the leadership of another guerrilla priest, Father Manuel Pérez (nom de guerre: *el cura*, the priest). Pérez, who died of malaria in Cuba in 1998, was able to bridge the differences between the various ELN factions and developed new sources of revenue—in large part funds extorted from multinational oil companies with operations in northeastern Colombia. The ELN grew from 800 in 1986 to 3000 fighters in 1996,

---

[17]Maullin, pp. 41–48.

organized into five *frentes de guerra* (war fronts). By 2000, the ELN's strength was estimated at 3000 to 5000 fighters.[18]

Over half of the ELN fighting force is concentrated in the northeastern war front, in the region from the middle Magdalena valley to the Venezuelan border. This deployment corresponds to the ELN's strategy of influencing the Colombian oil industry, which is concentrated in this area. The area also constitutes a strategic corridor linking Bogotá and the highlands with the Atlantic coast and with Venezuela to the east. The northwestern war front, with about 20 percent of the ELN force, operates in the mountains of Antioquia. The ELN has come under pressure in this area from FARC units that are disputing control of territory and resources and from paramilitaries who have mounted an aggressive challenge to both the ELN and the FARC in northwestern Colombia. The northern war front is active on the Atlantic coast and in the ELN's traditional stronghold in the San Lucas Mountains, in the southern part of the department of Bolívar. The two other, small war fronts are the southwestern, with some units operating in Nariño, Cauca, Huila, and Tolima; and the central, which includes an urban "nucleus" in Bogotá.[19]

OTHER GUERRILLA GROUPS

The FARC and the ELN are the dominant but not the only guerrilla groups active in Colombia. There are smaller groups that operate independently. The People's Liberation Army (Ejército Popular de Liberación, EPL) was organized in the 1960s as an anti-Moscow Maoist guerrilla group in remote parts of Antioquia and Córdoba, where land title disputes and physical isolation from the rest of Colombia provided seedbeds for revolutionary activity.[20] In 1984, the EPL, together with other guerrilla groups, signed a cease-fire with the government of President Betancur but resumed armed activities a year later. It suffered major losses in the counter-insurgency campaigns of the late 1980s. In 1990, the majority agreed to a peace settlement with the Colombian government, but a dissident faction decided to

---

[18]Rangel, p. 12; Echandía, pp. 51–57.

[19]Echandía, pp. 55–56.

[20]Maullin, pp. 48–49.

continue the struggle. The EPL dissidents were dealt a hard blow in 1994 when the Colombian army captured their leader Francisco Caraballo and 14 other senior cadres. Of 13 original EPL fronts, only four remain active. The EPL currently has several hundred fighters, with the largest component in the department of Chocó, near the Panamanian border.[21]

Other smaller groups, referred to as *disidencias* or dissidents, include the People's Revolutionary Army (Ejército Revolucionario del Pueblo, ERP), the Guevarist Revolutionary Army (Ejército Revolucionario Guevarista, ERG), and the Jaime Bateman Cayon group.

SOURCES OF GUERRILLA INCOME: LINKS TO THE DRUG TRADE

Recent research has sought to establish a tie between civil conflict and the ability of rebel groups to derive income from commodities.[22] Colombia is a classic case of guerrilla organizations that are able to capture enough resources to support the growth of their military forces.   According to Colombian government figures, in 1998 the various illegal organizations (guerrillas and paramilitaries) derived 620 billion pesos ($551 million) from the drug traffic, 350 billion pesos ($311 million) from extortion, and 265.5 billion pesos ($236 million) from kidnappings.[23]   According to Colombian analysts, the FARC and the ELN together account for 20 to 30 percent of all of the kidnappings that take place in the world.[24]

As shown in Table 3.1, over half of the FARC fronts were linked to (meaning derive income from and protect) the drug trade. The FARC has a precise schedule of fees, called *gramaje*, for protection and services to drug producers and smugglers. As of October 1999, the FARC fees (in U.S. dollars) were: production of basic paste, $15.70/kilo; chlorhydrate of cocaine, $52.60/kilo; protection of laboratories, $5263 each; protection of coca fields, $52.60/hectare; protection of

---

[21]Echandía, pp. 57–60.

[22]Paul Collier and Anke Hoeffler.

[23]Colombian armed forces briefing, March 2000.

[24]Rangel, p. 31.

Table 3.1

Links of Illegal Armed Groups to the Illicit Drug Trade

Units	FARC	ELN	AUC[a]
Total	61	41	19
Linked to drug trade	32	7	8

SOURCE: Colombian armed forces briefing, March 2000.

[a]United Self-Defense Forces (paramilitaries).

poppy fields, $4210/hectare; security of landing strips, $2631 each; cocaine shipments, $10.50/kilo; river transportation of precursor chemicals, 20 percent of shipment value; international drug flights, $5263 each; and domestic drug flights, $2631 each.[25]

In contrast to the FARC, the ELN manifested some reluctance to exploit the resources of the illegal drug trade. According to Colombian government figures, only one sixth of the ELN fronts are linked to the drug trade (see Table 3.1). However, after *el cura* Pérez' death, those who argue for a more "pragmatic" approach to drugs appear to be gaining ground within the ELN.[26]

Some Colombian analysts believe that although hard evidence is lacking it would be prudent to assume that the guerrillas have saved a substantial part of their income as a strategic financial reserve that would be available to sustain an escalation of the conflict.[27] In any event, the development of these sources of funding has broadened the range of strategic options available to the guerrillas.

OTHER SOURCES OF GUERRILLA INCOME

Before the development of the linkages between the guerrilla groups and the drug trade in the 1980s, the guerrillas derived most of their income from kidnappings and "revolutionary taxes," a thinly disguised form of extortion.[28] At the beginning of 2000 some 3000

---

[25]Colombian armed forces briefing, March 2000.

[26]Rangel, pp. 61–63.

[27]Rangel, p. 31.

[28]Or, as Spencer points out, not so thinly disguised, since the consequences of not paying are death, destruction of property, or kidnapping for ransom. Spencer also

people were being held for ransom, mostly by the guerrilla groups. Some 1559 people were kidnapped, including 126 children, in the first six months of 2000 alone.[29] A statistical survey of kidnappings in the 1987–1997 period shows that most of the kidnappings occurred in the agricultural and cattle-raising areas in the eastern part of the country and that the majority of the victims were cattle ranchers, farmers, and merchants, but the threat is very much felt in the cities, prompting an exodus of professional and business people. It is estimated that from 1991 to 1996 the guerrilla groups derived 788 billion pesos, or 22 percent of their total income, from kidnappings.[30]

Kidnappings are also used for propaganda purposes and to intimidate political and civil leaders. In some cases, the victims are high-profile individuals, including members of the Colombian Congress and former ministers.[31] Lower-level officials, especially mayors and municipal council members, are particularly vulnerable to kidnapping and the threat of kidnapping, assassination, and other intimidation tactics. Guerrillas and illegal self-defense groups avail themselves of these tactics to gain control of local governments and tap into revenues available to local authorities as the result of decentralization reform in the 1980s and 1990s. As discussed in the following chapter, as the guerrillas or illegal self-defense forces gain control of towns and rural areas, they also gain control of local government payrolls, infrastructure funds, and other sources of income.[32]

---

points out that kidnappings and extortion serve as a means of political control. Personal communication, December 2000.

[29]"Colombian, Venezuelan Business Leaders Flock to Miami," *Wall Street Journal*, August 30, 2000; "Kidnapped," in "Colombia: War Without End," www.cnn.com/SPECIAL/2000/colombia.

[30]Edgard Trujillo and Martha Elena Badel, "Los costos económicos de la criminalidad y la violencia en Colombia: 1991–96," cited in Echandía, p. 123.

[31]Former Conservative minister Argelino Durán Quintero was kidnapped and killed by a dissident faction of the EPL in March 1992; Representative Rodrigo Turbay Cote was kidnapped by the FARC in July 1996 and drowned while in FARC custody in May 1997; Representative Julio Bahamón Vanegas was kidnapped by the FARC in February 1997.

[32]For a more detailed discussion of this aspect of guerrilla strategy, see Chapter Five.

THE ARMS PIPELINE

These resources have enabled the guerrillas—primarily the FARC—to develop an arms pipeline that delivers assault rifles; heavy machine guns; 60mm, 81mm, and 82mm mortars; rocket-propelled grenades; and other military equipment, spare parts, and ammunition. The guerrillas are believed to possess shoulder-launched surface-to-air missiles, although they have not been used to date, and have reportedly upgraded their communications with Japanese and European encryption technology and voice scramblers.[33]

Central America was and remains a major source of the weapons smuggled into Colombia (see Figure 3.2). The arms are bought in El Salvador and Nicaragua from the stockpiles left from the Central American civil wars of the 1980s and smuggled through Panama to Colombia: by sea to the Colombian side of the Gulf of Urabá or on the Pacific side to the Gulf of San Miguel, or by land through a logistical bridge of 40 to 50 "trochas" or footpaths through the Darien gap (50 miles of triple-canopy jungle) between Panama and Colombia. The same infrastructure is used to smuggle drugs out of Colombia.[34]

According to a report in the Nicaraguan press, FARC representatives obtained 16 SA-16, SA-14, and SA-7 missiles from Sandinista stockpiles in May 1999.[35] The FARC has also secured rifles and ammunition from Venezuelan army stockpiles. (The capture of some of these weapons, with Venezuelan markings, by the Colombian army in the summer of 2000 led to an angry exchange between Colombian and Venezuelan officials.)[36] Explosives, uniforms, and other military supplies are smuggled across the border from Ecuador.[37]

---

[33]Douglas Farah, "Colombian Rebels' Arsenal Grows as Cocaine Sales Increase in E. Europe," *Washington Post*, November 4, 1999.

[34]Discussions with Panamanian security experts, Panama City, April 2000.

[35]"Confirmados nexos entre Sandinistas y las FARC," *La Noticia*, Managua, September 19, 1999.

[36]"El silencio sobre las armas," *Venezuela Analítica*, July 24, 2000.

[37]Discussion with a senior Colombian military officer, September 2000.

RAND*MR1339-3.2*

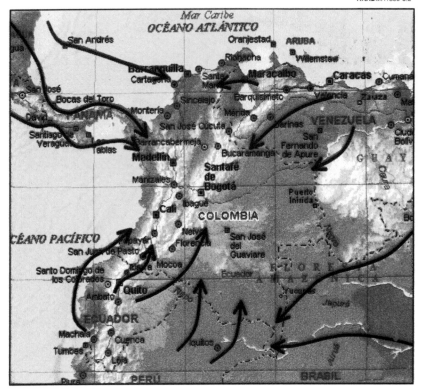

SOURCE: Colombian Ministry of Defense.

Figure 3.2—Arms Smuggling Routes into Colombia

There has also been an inflow of weapons from Eastern Europe and the former Soviet Union, possibly as the result of linkages between Colombian drug smugglers and guerrillas and Russian criminal syndicates. A shipment of 10,000 AK-47 assault rifles was air-dropped into FARC-controlled territory in eastern Colombia from chartered cargo planes that were supposedly transporting the rifles to Peru from Jordan. (It subsequently was alleged that the then-powerful chief of the Peruvian National Intelligence Service, Vladimiro Montesinos, had masterminded the transaction.)[38]

SUPPORTING NETWORKS AND INFORMATION-AGE WARFARE

The guerrillas draw political strength and sustenance from a robust network of supporting organizations, both in Colombia and overseas. Multiorganizational networks aided the insurgencies in El Salvador and Guatemala and the Sandinistas in Nicaragua in the 1980s, but have assumed a larger role with the information revolution of the 1990s and particularly with the development of the Internet.

Information warfare techniques were successfully employed by the Zapatistas in Mexico to paralyze the Mexican government's response to the armed insurgency in Chiapas.[39] Although the Colombian insurgency remains much closer to a traditional guerrilla war than to the "netwar" that the Zapatistas waged in Mexico, the FARC and the ELN have developed a wide range of multiorganizational supporting networks both in Colombia and overseas. The strategic objectives of these networks is to restrict the actions of the Colombian state and its agencies and to deny it international support. For example, an open letter e-mailed in the spring of 2000 to European Union governments and organizations opposed the Pastrana government's efforts to generate international support for Plan Colombia. The signatories included European human rights organizations, "committees

---

[38]"Neighbors Worry About Colombian Aid," *New York Times*, August 25, 2000. According to information provided by Colombian military sources, the rifles were air-dropped along the IL-76 flight path in the remote department of Vichada. STRATFOR.com Global Intelligence Update (www.stratfor.com/home/giu/DAILY.asp) reported on September 18, 2000, that the arms-smuggling ring was detected in August 1999 by Colombia and the United States after the CIA tracked the serial numbers of AK-47 rifles captured from the FARC by the Colombian army. The CIA reportedly confirmed that the rifles had been sold by Jordan to Peru. Further investigation led to the brothers Frank and Jose Aybar Cancho, whose uncle, Manuel Aybar, was the longtime head of Montesinos' personal security detail.

[39]See David Ronfeldt, John Arquilla, Graham E. Fuller, and Melissa Fuller, *The Zapatista Social Netwar in Mexico*, RAND, MR-994-A, 1998.

of solidarity" with Colombia in Italy, Belgium, France, and Great Britain, and Colombian unions and political, environmental, and religious groups.[40]

Control of the "zona de despeje" or demilitarized zone has amplified the FARC's ability to conduct such information operations. The FARC has held a series of public conferences on social and economic problems with representatives of labor, business, and civil society organizations in San Vicente del Caguán. These conferences and visits by international dignitaries, such as New York Stock Exchange Chairman Grasso, were widely reported in the Colombian and international media and helped the FARC to publicize its demands, criticize the government, and engage influential audiences.

The FARC scored a significant political victory at the end of June 2000 when diplomats from Europe, Canada, Japan, and the United Nations traveled to the FARC-controlled zone to discuss crop eradication and human rights with FARC leaders. The visit underscored the differences between the U.S. and European approaches to the Colombian crisis (discussed in Chapter Six). After the discussions, the diplomats attended a forum with several hundred small farmers from the area who denounced the U.S. and Colombian government counter-narcotics policies.[41]

Activities such as these enhance the guerrillas' perceived legitimacy, diminish the stature of the government in Bogotá, and complicate the Colombian government's ability to secure international support. As will be seen in the following chapter, this is part of an integrated FARC strategy to increase its leverage and influence over Colombia's future.

---

[40]E-mail, "Pen letter to the countries of the group of support for peace in Colombia."

[41]"Diplomats Parlay with Colombian Rebels," *Washington Post*, June 30, 2000.

Chapter Four

GUERRILLA STRATEGY

GRAND STRATEGY

A review of FARC operations during the 1990s suggests that the FARC is implementing the strategic plan laid out at its Seventh Conference in May 1982.[1] In an interview published in *El Tiempo* on March 2, 1999, FARC leader Marulanda observed that the FARC's military advances had brought the struggle to a new stage, in which the Colombian government had been forced to agree to negotiations. Marulanda stated that the FARC would not repeat "past errors," such as the negotiations in the mid-1980s that led to the demobilization of the M-19 guerrilla movement, and would continue the struggle "until victory."[2]

Colombian analysts believe that the strategic objectives of the FARC are:

First, to consolidate its control of coca-growing regions in the southern and eastern part of the country. Control of the resources in these areas enables the guerrillas to build up their military capabilities and push into other areas.

---

[1]The official FARC history states that this conference, which designated the FARC as a "People's Army," gave the movement, for the first time, "a clear operational and strategic concept," requiring a readjustment of all of its command structure. See "Las FARC: 30 años de lucha por la paz, democracia y soberanía," http://www.tierra.ucsd.edu/farc-ep/Nuestra_historia/.

[2]*El Tiempo*, Bogotá, January 18, 2000.

Second, to expand the theater of operations to the entire country, so as to force the government to disperse its forces and reduce its ability to regain the military initiative. At the same time, the guerrillas seek to expand into economically strategic areas, such as the middle Magdalena valley and the central highlands. To do this, the FARC is striving to control a number of strategic corridors that link the FARC's base in the *zona de despeje* to the Pacific coast and to northeastern Colombia and the Venezuelan border and permit the rapid movement of troops, arms, and supplies across the country. (See Figure 4.1.) Some of the most intense fighting over the past two years has been over control of these corridors.

Third, to isolate the capital, Bogotá, and other major cities. Perched at 6000 feet on the western slope of the eastern cordillera of the Andes, Bogotá is dependent on a few easily interdicted roads for land communications with the external world.[3] The FARC and the ELN regularly sever road communications between the capital and the Atlantic coast, the Amazonian region, and the eastern plains.[4]

In the last several years, the FARC has established seven new fronts in areas close to Bogotá, responding to both its strategic plan and to the development of poppy fields on the eastern slope of the Andes, which provide a source of income for the new FARC fronts.

The final stage in the FARC's strategy would be a move to large-scale offensive operations, culminating in a general uprising.[5] To this end, the FARC has been building urban support networks in Bogotá and

---

[3]These are the Pan-American Highway, south and west to Girardot and Ibagué, and north to Tunja, Cúcuta, and the Venezuelan border; the road west across the Magdalena river to Caldas; and the road across the mountains to Villavicencia and the eastern plains.

[4]In a series of attacks on the road network in April 2000, the ELN blocked the Pan-American Highway south of Cali, the road from Pasto, the capital of Nariño department, to the Pacific port of Tumaco; blew up a bridge on the Bogotá-Medellín highway; and cut road communications leading to the northeastern cities of Barrancabermeja, Bucaramanga, and Cúcuta "Primer muerto por 'paro armado,'" *El Tiempo*, April 11, 2000

[5]The Salvadoran Farabundo Martí National Liberation Front (FMLN) pursued a similar three-stage strategy, culminating in the failed "final offensive" of November 1989. After the failure of the offensive, the FMLN concluded that there was no viable alternative to a political settlement.

RAND MR1339-4.1

Figure 4.1—Main Theaters of Operations

other cities. Beginning in 1996, the FARC inaugurated a new phase of the war, involving multifront attacks on military objectives and use of 60mm and 81mm mortars and homemade bombs fired from a tube, known as cylinder bombs.

These attacks inflicted major defeats on the Colombian army. On August 30, 1996, the FARC launched a surprise night attack on the military base at Las Delicias, in Putumayo. After 15 hours of fighting, the base was destroyed. Colombian army losses were 54 dead, 17 wounded, and 60 captured.[6] In March 1998 at El Billar, in southern Caquetá, the FARC annihilated an elite army unit, the 52nd counter-guerrilla battalion of the Colombian army's 3rd Mobile Brigade. The battalion had been stationed for six weeks in the town of Peña Colorada, deep in guerrilla-controlled territory, before receiving orders to conduct operations against the FARC infrastructure in the lower Caguan river. Spies and local sympathizers provided the FARC with intelligence on the battalion's strength and movements, while the Colombian army commanders were unaware of massing guerrilla forces in the vicinity. On March 2, a force of 600–800 FARC guerrillas sealed off escape routes and attacked the battalion in hilly and forested terrain. Despite the Colombian air force's deployment of Kfir, Mirage V, TAC-47, and OV-10 aircraft, overcast skies prevented the effective use of air power in support of the beleaguered battalion. An attempted airborne landing was aborted when the guerrillas covered landing clearances with antiair ambushes. By the time reinforcements were able to land, on March 4, the battalion had been destroyed as an effective fighting force, with a loss of 107 of its 154 men.[7] In August 1998, FARC guerrillas attacked and destroyed an antidrug base at Miraflores, in southeastern Guaviare. In November 1998, 1000 FARC guerrillas overran Mitu, a provincial capital near the

---

[6]The FARC has released some of the soldiers captured in combat, but has held most as chips to pressure the Colombian government to accede to guerrilla demands. Relatives and friends of the captured soldiers have periodically demonstrated in Bogotá demanding that the government secure their freedom. As of October 2000, the FARC held 528 soldiers and policemen. See "El canje," *Semana,* October 16–22, 2000.

[7]David Spencer notes that the soldiers were issued only 280 rounds of ammunition each and were low on rifle grenades and batteries for radio-frequency scanners. Night-vision goggles, smoke grenades, and illumination flares were left behind because they were considered unnecessary weight. Three of the four battalion radios were put out of action in the initial guerrilla attack. David Spencer, "FARC Warfare Strategy and Tactics 1996–1999," unpublished manuscript.

Brazilian border. The Colombian army recaptured Mitu only after the Brazilians granted permission for Colombian troops to land in Brazilian bases across the border.

Control of the *zona de despeje*, the 42,139 square kilometers in southern Colombia evacuated by the Colombian government as a condition for negotiations, constitutes a major strategic asset for the FARC. The FARC uses the zone as a sanctuary from which to launch operations, rest and refit its forces, move drugs and arms, and even hold prisoners and hostages. The FARC used the area as a base to launch a multifront attack involving 4000 fighters in July 1999 against the military bases and towns in the departments of Meta, Guaviare, Huila, Putumayo, and Caquetá.[8]

The FARC again launched major attacks in the region around Bogotá after the Christmas truce of December 1999. In early January 2000, some 800 FARC guerrillas attacked military and police positions in the towns of Une, Quetame, and Guayabetal 60 kilometers south of Bogotá, and cut off land communications between Bogotá and Villavicencio, the capital of the department of Meta and the largest city in the eastern plains.[9] In the spring and summer of 2000 the tempo of multifront FARC operations slowed, although attacks on isolated police posts and infrastructure targets continued.

The frequency of mass guerrilla attacks in 2000 diminished in relation to the 1997–1998 period, which Colombia military sources attribute to the increased Colombian use of air power after the battle of Mitu (see the appendix). In addition, the new Colombian military leadership, which took the reins of the Colombian armed forces in 1998, understood the need to move away from a defensive posture and to undertake offensive operations. This led to the establishment of a 5000-strong rapid deployment force (RDF) under the operational control of the army high command.[10] In the first six months of 2000, the armed forces conducted 1808 counter-insurgency actions, resulting in 504 insurgents killed in action, compared to 855 actions and

---

[8]"Operación independencia," *Eventos*, República de Colombia, Ejército Nacional, 1999.

[9]"Las FARC querían aislar a Bogotá," *La Nación*, January 17, 2000.

[10]Spencer and Noss, p. 7.

364 insurgents killed in action in 1999.[11]   In Operation Annihilator II, in September 2000, troops of the Colombian 13th Brigade cleared the FARC from the Sumapaz area, a strategic corridor extending from the eastern plains to the outskirts of Bogotá.[12]

Some analysts believe that the FARC is using this time to train and refit its forces for a resumption of offensive operations at a later date.[13]   There is no question, however, that the FARC has the capability to return to the offensive on a large scale when it judges that the strategic situation is favorable.[14]   The action at Dabeida in October 2000, when FARC guerrillas killed 54 soldiers and policemen in heavy fighting, illustrates the limitations of the government's reliance on helicopters for mobility.

The battle developed when 600 guerrillas from the FARC's northwestern block attacked and captured the town of Dabeida, astride a critical corridor between the Urabá region of Antioquia and the department of Chocó on the Pacific coast. Another 400 FARC, ELN, and Guevarist Revolutionary Army guerrillas captured the town of Bagadó, in Chocó. The FARC's strategic objective was to open a logistics corridor to the Pacific coast. The immediate tactical objective, however, was to lure the army reaction force into a prepared kill zone—a tactic that the FARC had been developing since 1996. The

---

[11]"Cómo va la guerra," *Cambio*, Bogotá, June 19–26, 2000.

[12]"Los teatros de la guerra," *Semana*, October 9–15, 2000.

[13]David Spencer notes that there is a seasonal pattern to FARC offensives, which tend to occur at mid-year and at the end or the beginning of the year. Time in between is used to prepare for further attacks. The Colombian army claims that December 2000 FARC attacks were blunted. Personal communication from David Spencer, December 2000.

[14]FARC second-in-command Jorge Briceño reportedly stated that the FARC was in a position to seize the departmental capitals of Villavicencio or Florencia but refrained while it was engaged in peace negotiations. Penhaul, p. 3. At a conference in Washington on September 27, 2000, the mayor of Quidbó, capital of Chocó department, noted that there were three FARC fronts, two ELN fronts, and two AUC (paramilitary) fronts operating in the department and that it was only a matter of time before Quidbó fell into the hands of subversive groups. Presentation by Arnobio Córdoba, mayor of Quibdó, at Georgetown University and National Endowment for Democracy Conference on "Local Government Amidst the Armed Conflict: The Experience of Colombian Mayors," Georgetown University, Washington, D.C., September 27, 2000.

kill zone was surrounded by deep rifle pits connected to bunkers with overhead cover.[15]

The Colombian army 4th Brigade responded by dispatching 350 Special Forces troops to recapture Dabeida. The troops were to be transported in three sorties of five helicopters to an area six kilometers from the town. One of the helicopters was grounded because of mechanical problems; another one, a UH-60 Black Hawk, crashed after being hit by guerrilla fire, killing all 22 soldiers and crew members aboard. The three other helicopters were damaged by hostile fire and returned to their base after landing some 80 troops, who then came under fire from superior guerrilla forces. The Colombian commanders requested replacement helicopters for the damaged helicopters used in the operation, but they did not arrive until nightfall. The reinforcements did not make contact with the surviving troops until the following morning. By then, only 32 were still alive.[16]

The ELN has generally avoided military confrontations and has pursued an "economic strategy" consisting of attacks on the power grid and the communications infrastructure, "armed propaganda," kidnappings, and airplane hijackings; this strategy reflects the organization's military weakness in relation to the other actors in the conflict. Although the ELN's long-term political objectives are compatible with those of the FARC, the two organizations have been competing for local control—there were reports of executions of ELN commanders in January 2000 by members of the FARC's 9th front in Antioquia.[17] On the other hand, FARC units have joined forces with the ELN in southern Bolívar against the advance of the paramilitaries and, as noted above, in the capture of Dabeida.[18]

---

[15]Spencer notes that at the battles of Puerto Rico, Puerto Lleras, and Vega Larga, the FARC set up kill zones with thousands of guerrillas and waited for the army to fall into the trap. In each of those cases, the army detected the kill zones and avoided falling into them; in Dabeida, the army fell right into the trap.

[16]"Colombian Troops Take Losses in 3-day Battle," *Washington Post*, October 21, 2000.

[17]"Guerra de guerrillas entre FARC and ELN," *El Tiempo*, January 9, 2000. The ELN denounced the killings, but noted that it did not consider the incident the result of FARC policy but mistakes by individual FARC commanders.

[18]"Encuentro en Madrid," *Cambio*, June 19–26, 2000.

The ELN's short-term objective is control of its own demilitarized zone and equal status with the FARC in the peace negotiations. In May 2000, the Pastrana administration agreed in principle to establish a demilitarized zone for the ELN in the southern Bolívar department. Unlike the zone conceded to the FARC, which is located in a remote part of Colombia, the zone proposed for the ELN is a strategically important area, bordering on the Magdalena river, the country's major river artery, and the oil-refining complex at Barrancabermeja. Moreover, for the past two years the area has been under the control of militias associated with the United Self-Defense Forces of Colombia (AUC).[19] As discussed in Chapter Seven, the plan to establish an ELN zone in the area was strongly opposed by the local authorities and population and, as of this writing, had not been implemented.

CONTROLLING THE GRASS ROOTS: THE LOCAL DIMENSION OF GUERRILLA STRATEGY

All of the guerrilla groups (as well as the paramilitaries) are seeking to expand their control of the grass-roots levels of government, that is, municipalities or townships (*municipios*) and rural areas (*corregimientos*). According to the most complete set of statistical data on violence and armed conflict in Colombia, the guerrilla presence has spread from 173 municipalities in 1985 to 437 in 1991 and to 622 in 1995, out of a total of approximately 1050 municipalities.[20] Figures 4.2 and 4.3 show the expansion of the area of FARC activity from 1986–1987 to 1996–1997.[21]

The growth of the guerrilla presence in the country's agricultural backbone—the coffee-growing departments of central Colombia and

---

[19]"Paramilitary Chief Opposes Peace Plan," *Washington Times,* May 16, 2000.

[20]Echandía, p. 60.

[21]Areas of guerrilla presence are defined as areas where guerrilla groups have carried out armed activities, including attacks on military and police units, and harassment, sabotage, and attacks on towns, government installations, and infrastructure. Darker areas denote greater guerrilla activity. Some caution needs to be used in interpreting the maps because all of the municipalities where guerrilla activity was registered are represented, possibly overestimating the geographic scope of the guerrilla presence. Nevertheless, the maps provide a gauge of the spread of guerrilla activity during this ten-year period.

the densely populated commercial agriculture areas—is particularly alarming. According to Echandía's figures, the guerrilla presence in the coffee-growing region increased from 2 percent of the municipalities in 1985 to 53 percent in 1995. In commercial agriculture areas, the guerrilla presence went from 13 percent of the municipalities in 1985 to 71 percent in 1995.[22]

Guerrilla influence remains strongest in regions of "internal colonization" (west of the eastern cordillera) and "border colonization" (east of the eastern cordillera). This is Colombia's agricultural frontier, the vast areas where migrants from the more established agricultural areas in Colombia have moved to find land. This is also where most of Colombia's coca is produced. The guerrilla presence in internal colonization areas increased from 62 percent in 1985 to 93 percent in 1995; in the border colonization areas, it rose from 44 percent in 1985 to 81 percent in 1995.[23]

There are two stages of guerrilla infiltration and takeover of localities. The first stage is the arrival of a group of cadres charged with reconnoitering the terrain, identifying sources of income, and laying the groundwork for a guerrilla administration. This is followed by the arrival of a so-called public order commission—armed guerrillas who seek to gain public sympathy by imposing their own version of law and order, which generally involves actions against local criminals or other unpopular individuals.[24] Once the guerrillas gain control of a locality, it becomes a source of support—financial and logistical— and a springboard for further expansion.

The Colombian government's policy of decentralization, which devolved authority and resources to local governments, made the latter even juicier targets for the illegal armed groups. Municipal governments experienced an increase in resources from 2.6 percent of GDP in 1980 to 5.5 percent of GDP in 1994.[25] Through their control or links to local officials, the guerrillas are able to tap into these

---

[22]Echandía, p. 60.

[23]Echandía, p. 61. Definitions of these areas can be found in Echandía, pp. 31–42.

[24]Rangel, pp. 40–41.

[25]World Bank, "Local Government Capacity in Colombia: Beyond Technical Assistance," Washington, D.C., 1995, p. 1. *Municipios* have access to additional resources from the national level through the system of cofinancing funds.

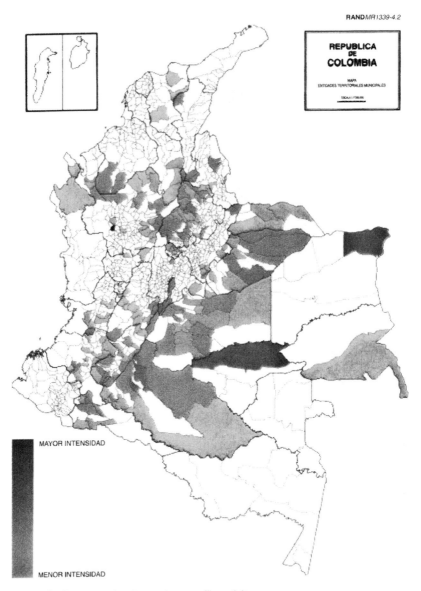

RAND*MR1339-4.2*

MAYOR INTENSIDAD

MENOR INTENSIDAD

NOTE: Darker areas denote greater guerrilla activity.
SOURCE: Echandía, p. 95.

Figure 4.2—Areas of Expansion of FARC Activity: 1986–1987

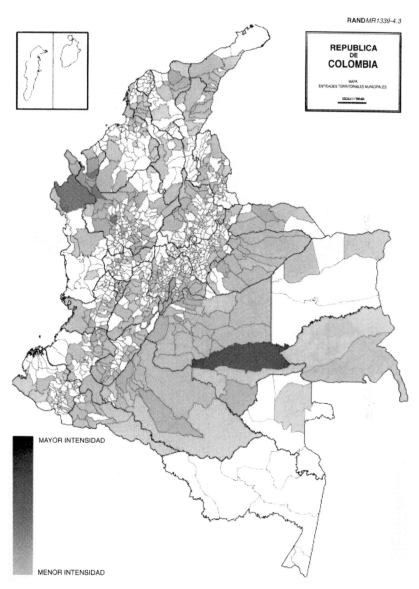

RAND*MR1339-4.3*

NOTE: Darker areas denote greater guerrilla activity.
SOURCE: Echandía, p. 117.

Figure 4.3—Areas of Expansion of FARC Activity: 1996–1997

resources. The guerrillas, in effect, replicate the functions and methods of the traditional political bosses or *gamonales*—they "recommend" individuals for jobs in the local bureaucracy, retain part of their earnings as "contributions," demand payments for the award of public works contracts, and collect a cut of public expenditures.[26]

Small towns and rural areas are, for the most part, highly vulnerable to guerrilla infiltration. According to official figures, there is no police presence in one fourth of the country's *municipios* or *corregimientos*.[27] Small and isolated police and military posts simply become targets of opportunity for guerrilla attacks: In the first half of 2000, the guerrillas carried out 176 attacks on police posts.[28] In these attacks, as noted above, the guerrillas typically use homemade propane cylinders filled with explosives, napalm, or tear gas launched from improvised mortars fashioned from 55-gallon drums or larger canisters. These are highly inaccurate devices that often result in casualties among the civilian population and severe damage to the town that is being attacked.

The experience of the town of Alpujarra, in southern Tolima, illustrates the vulnerability of exposed towns in contested areas. On November 6, 1998, a 300-strong FARC force overwhelmed the town's small police garrison; Colombian army reinforcements did not arrive in time. On December 12, 1999, the town was again attacked in a FARC general offensive in Tolima. On March 20, 2000, guerrillas attacked a nearby communications tower that relayed signals to and from the departments of Tolima, Huila, Caquetá, Vaupez, and Putumayo. The guerrillas also attacked the police station, but were driven off by the Colombian air force. On May 3, the guerrillas dynamited the communications tower, leaving the town without communications. On July 12, there was another violent guerrilla attack—within a two-hour period, the guerrillas blanketed the town with 35 home-

---

[26]Presentation by Gilberto Toro, Executive Secretary, *Federación Colombiana de Municipios*, at Georgetown University and National Endowment for Democracy,Conference on "Local Government Amidst the Armed Conflict: The Experience of Colombian Mayors"; see also Rangel, pp. 34–36.

[27]There is no police presence in 254 *municipios* or *corregimientos*. Colombian armed forces briefing, March 2000.

[28]"Cómo va la guerra," *Cambio*, Bogotá, June 19–26, 2000.

made propane cylinder bombs.[29] As a result, many of the inhabitants fled to the provincial capital, Ibagué, which, like other Colombian cities, has been overrun by large numbers of displaced persons.

Local officials and political and civic leaders are very much at the mercy of the armed groups. Prior to the October 1997 regional elections, which the guerrillas attempted to block, 110 candidates and political activists were murdered, 244 were kidnapped, 359 mayoral candidates were forced to withdraw, and 22 *municipios* were left without candidates. Two hundred mayors were declared "military targets"—candidates for assassination by guerrillas or paramilitaries.[30] Lack of basic security is at the root of the dysfunctional nature of Colombian governmental and judicial institutions.

---

[29]Presentation by Aura Ospina, mayor of Alpujarra, at Georgetown University and National Endowment for Democracy Conference on "Local Government Amidst the Armed Conflict: The Experience of Colombian Mayors," Georgetown University, Washington, D.C., September 27, 2000.

[30]"La democracia en peligro: los alcaldes como objectivo militar," Centro de Información sobre el Desarrollo de la Democracia en Colombia (CIDEC), August 2000, www.cidec.org.

Chapter Five

THE ILLEGAL SELF-DEFENSE GROUPS: CAUSE OR SYMPTOM OF THE DISORDER?

ORIGINS, CHARACTERISTICS, AND ORGANIZATION

The guerrillas are not alone in using violence to control territory. As their presence and power have expanded, so have the illegal self-defense organizations, also known as paramilitaries, dedicated to eradicating the insurgency. The *autodefensas,* or self-defense groups, are the third party in Colombia's three-sided civil conflict.[1] Local armed self-defense groups have developed throughout Colombia's history with varying degrees of government sanction during periods of turmoil and armed conflict. During the period of *la violencia,* many localities organized armed formations to defend themselves against bandits and political armed bands.

In the current conflict, the self-defense groups emerged in reaction to the guerrillas in areas where the state was unable to provide security to the population. Some originated as civil defense units organized by the Colombian government in the 1960s and 1970s. A 1964 civil defense law allowed the creation of civil defense units to support the army in counter-insurgency. Some were private security forces funded by landowners and businessmen. Others were the

---

[1]The term paramilitaries is an unsatisfactory rubric to describe the *autodefensas* although it has gained widespread currency. The term more properly describes elements of the security forces with some military capabilities such as the Italian *carabinieri* or the Spanish Civil Guard. It has no particular descriptive value in referring to the *autodefensas* and (perhaps intentionally) might convey the implication of quasi-official status.

bodyguards of drug traffickers and other criminals. In the 1980s, some of the legal self-defense units developed links with criminal elements, including drug-trafficking networks, and have become indistinguishable from criminal organizations. As the result of the involvement of some of these groups in criminal activities, the self-defense units were outlawed in 1987. Nevertheless, the self-defense groups did not lay down their arms. In fact, they continued to grow and expand, now outside of any government control.[2]

Convivir units represent another model of self-defense organizations. *Convivir,* originated in Antioquia in the early 1990s and based on the neighborhood watch concept, was deliberately set up to avoid the appearance of the outlawed paramilitary groups. *Convivir* was a way of involving people in the struggle against the subversive organizations without organizing them as militias. These groups performed intelligence functions for the security forces and became the targets of guerrilla attack. Unlike the *rondas campesinas,* the Peruvian community self-defense militias that played a critical role in the defeat of the Shining Path insurgency, the *Convivir* groups were not allowed to carry rifles or heavier weapons needed to defend themselves effectively against guerrilla attacks.[3] They could carry only side arms. In the mid-1990s, the Colombian government moved to dismantle the self-defense groups. The *Convivir* groups were declared illegal, allegedly on the grounds that some of them had begun to arm themselves unlawfully and had morphed into "illegal" self-defense groups.

The illegal self-defense organizations are far less cohesive than are the guerrillas, although in recent years the groups have clustered under an umbrella organization, the *Autodefensas Unidas de Colombia* (United Self-Defense Forces of Colombia), or AUC. The AUC brought to these groups some degree of central coordination, funding, and a coherent doctrine. There are currently some 8000 fighters in the AUC and a number of regional organizations, including the *Autodefensas Campesinas de Córdoba y Urabá, Autodefensas*

---

[2]Personal communication from Spencer, December 2000.

[3]By contrast, the Peruvian government distributed 10,000 rifles to the *rondas* by 1993. Cynthia McClintock, "The Decimation of Peru's Sendero Luminoso," in Cynthia J. Arnson, *Comparative Peace Processes in Latin America,* Woodrow Wilson Center Press, Washington, D.C., 1999, p. 236.

Casanare, Autodefensas de Santander y Sur del César, and the *Autodefensas del Putumayo Bloque Sur.*[4]

The first of these organizations, the *Autodefensas Campesinas de Córdoba y Urabá* (ACCU) was established by the brothers Fidel and Carlos Castaño in Urabá to avenge the kidnapping and murder of their father by the FARC in 1981. Carlos Castaño became the AUC leader after Fidel's death in an encounter with the FARC in 1996. In that same year, Castaño organized the AUC as a vehicle for a nationwide expansion of paramilitary activities. With better funding and equipment, the AUC formations have evolved from local militias to full-time professional fighters capable of offensive operations. From their base areas in Córdoba and the Urabá region in Antioquia on the Atlantic coast, the groups have contested control of a band of territory from northern Antioquia to the eastern plains.[5] They have succeeded in displacing the FARC from the area around San José del Guaviare, near the Venezuelan border, and from the area of Puerto Asís in Putumayo, formerly guerrilla strongholds.

The strategy and tactics of the AUC mirror those of the guerrillas. The AUC is seeking to extend its control at the local level and to exercise political influence through the control or intimidation of local officials. Its strategy is to dispute control of the drug-producing areas where the guerrillas have their main sources of income.[6] For this reason, Guaviare, Putumayo, and Caquetá have become a major battleground in the struggle between the FARC and the AUC. In Florencia, the capital of Caquetá, 256 homicides were registered in a three-month period as the result of the FARC-AUC power struggle.[7]

Illegal self-defense groups are considered responsible for the majority of the reported mass killings by organized groups. It is estimated

---

[4]Colombian armed forces briefing March 2000; "Outlaw Unit Offers Help in Drug War," *Washington Times*, May 16, 2000.

[5]Rangel takes the view that the paramilitaries' military objective is to penetrate the FARC's strategic rear guard in the south and seize control of the area's cocaine industry. Rangel, pp. 49–50.

[6]Rangel, p. 50.

[7]Presentation by Lucrecia Murcia, mayor of Florencia, at Georgetown University and National Endowment for Democracy Conference on "Local Government Amidst the Armed Conflict: The Experience of Colombian Mayors," Washington, D.C., September 27, 2000.

that of 23,184 persons murdered by illegal armed organizations between 1988 and 1997, 3532 were killed by guerrillas and 19,652 by other organizations, which include illegal self-defense organizations, the drug cartels, and "private justice" groups.[8] In contested areas, AUC forces routinely execute alleged guerrilla sympathizers to instill fear and compel support among the local population. The AUC also engaged in large-scale attacks on villages suspected of supporting the guerrillas, in retaliation for guerrilla attacks, or to remove the guerrillas' support network.[9] The AUC acknowledges these massacres, but argues that the killings are conducted on the basis of intelligence on FARC collaborators, often provided by FARC deserters from the area. A well-informed observer of the Colombian military situation noted that there are in fact numerous FARC deserters in the AUC ranks, because of the harsh discipline imposed by the FARC and because the AUC offers protection from retaliation by their former comrades.[10]

Despite the atrocities attributed to them, the Colombian public views the illegal self-defense groups less unfavorably than the guerrillas. An October 1999 Yankelovich, Acevedo and Associates poll asked who were the greatest enemies of Colombia's welfare. Thirty-nine percent of the respondents chose the guerrillas, 9 percent common criminals, and 8 percent the paramilitaries. Twenty-three percent

---

[8]Echandía, p. 69. Echandía cautions that these figures, from the Colombian government's Departamento Administrativo de Seguridad (DAS) data, underestimate the real numbers. The annual number of murders in Colombia in this period ranges from 21,500 to over 28,000, or a rate of 73.58 to 86.05 per 100,000 inhabitants. Ibid., pp. 235–236.

[9]For instance, in January 1999, AUC men swept through villages in six departments and killed some 150 suspected guerrilla sympathizers in retaliation for a bloody FARC attack on the AUC headquarters at El Nudo de Paramillo in December 1998. *The Economist*, January 16, 1999.

[10]Guerrillas have been primarily responsible for the majority of all other types of human rights violations, including murders fewer than four persons, kidnappings, attacks on population centers, and acts of terrorism. See table in República de Colombia, Ministerio de Defensa Nacional, *La fuerza pública y los derechos humanos en Colombia*, Bogotá, March 2000, p. 14. Although there were some widely publicized massacres in 1999 and 2000, the trend in the number of mass murders (those involving four or more victims)—the type of crime often associated with the AUC—has been downward since 1990, as shown in Echandía, p. 71. Since there has not been a decrease in AUC activity in this time frame, this trend might reflect a decision by AUC leaders to avoid the type of high-profile atrocities that would further reduce their prospects of acceptance as legitimate political actors.

chose "others"; 19 percent "all of the above"; and 1 percent the armed forces.[11]

ALLEGATIONS OF COLLUSION WITH THE COLOMBIAN MILITARY

Cooperation, tacit or open, between the AUC and the Colombian army has repeatedly been alleged. The gunmen who carried out a massacre at the town of El Tigre in January 1999 were reported to have arrived in four trucks belonging to the army's 24th Brigade.[12] Guerrillas and human rights activists accuse the army and AUC of cooperating in activities against the rebels' civilian supporters. According to press reports, a number of senior paramilitary leaders in Putumayo previously served as noncommissioned officers (NCOs) or junior officers in the Colombian military.[13]

The diverse and changing nature of the self-defense groups makes it difficult to analyze their relationship with the Colombian military, particularly at the local level. The Colombian government has declared the battle against the illegal self-defense groups a strategic priority and has established the National Coordination Center to lead the fight against these groups.[14] According to Colombian government data, between 1997 and 1999, 76 members of illegal self-defense groups were killed in confrontations with the security forces and 705 were captured. In the same period, 2677 members of guerrilla organizations were killed and 3796 captured. The number of paramilitaries killed and captured represented, respectively, 1.36 percent and 12.63 percent of the total force. For the guerrillas, the proportions of personnel killed and captured were, respectively, 10.37 percent and 14.72 percent.

Colombian authorities point to the close ratios of captured paramilitaries and guerrillas as evidence of even-handedness. With regard to the disproportion in the ratios of those killed in action, the Colom-

---

[11]See table in *La fuerza pública y los derechos humanos en Colombia*, p. 29.

[12]*The Economist*, January 16, 1999.

[13]"Outlaw Unit Offers Help in Drug War," *Washington Times*, May 16, 2000.

[14]"Fight Against Illegal Self-Defenses," Colombian Ministry of Defense, 2000.

bian Ministry of Defense human rights report notes that the results could hardly have been different, given that the guerrillas are much more likely to seek confrontation with the armed forces than are the illegal self-defense forces.[15]

The Colombian authorities have also taken steps against officers accused of collaborating with paramilitaries or failing to prevent attacks on civilians. In July 2000, the Office of the Procurator General indicted four generals and a colonel for failing to take measures to prevent the killing of 18 villagers at Puerto Alvira, Meta, in May 1998.[16] One of the officers, Brigadier General Jaime Uscategui, former commander of the 7th Brigade, was subsequently found guilty by a military court-martial of failing to prevent an earlier massacre in Mapiripán, Meta, in which 30 people were murdered.[17] In October 2000, the Minister of Defense announced the dismissal of 388 officers and noncommissioned officers for human rights abuses, corruption, and other reasons, as part of an effort to improve the military's performance.[18]

LINKS TO THE DRUG TRADE

The extent of the income that the illegal self-defense groups derive from the narcotics trade is not known, but it is believed to be considerable. As noted in Table 3.1, eight of 19 squads associated with Carlos Castaño's AUC are considered by Colombian authorities to be linked to the drug trade. In a televised interview in March 2000, Cas-

---

[15]For instance, according to Colombian government data, of 115 attacks on population centers in 1999, 106 were carried out by guerrillas and nine by illegal self-defense forces. *La fuerza pública y los derechos humanos en Colombia*, pp. 20–21. Broken down by year, the data show an increase of the ratio of members of illegal self-defense forces killed in action to those in the total force from 0.25 percent in 1996 to about 5 percent in 1999, suggesting a tougher approach by the authorities.

[16]The army responded that two of the generals had left their commands in the area five months before the incident occurred, and that the nearest army troops were 100 km from the site and therefore could not have prevented the incident. "Cargos contra 4 generales por masacre de Puerto Alvira," *El Tiempo*, July 28, 2000.

[17]*Semana*, "General condenado," February 19–25, 2001.

[18]The officers and NCOs were dismissed pursuant to a decree signed by President Pastrana allowing the Minister of Defense to dismiss officers deemed unfit for duty; they were not charged with specific abuses. "Colombian Military Fires 388 in Human Rights Effort," *Washington Post*, October 17, 2000.

taño admitted that drug trafficking and taxation of peasants producing coca in Antioquia and Córdoba provided up to 70 percent of the financing for his forces (with the rest largely coming from extortion).[19] According to testimony of a U.S. Drug Enforcement Agency (DEA) official, the Castaño organization appears to be directly involved in processing cocaine and at least one of the paramilitary groups appears to be involved in exporting cocaine from Colombia.[20]

POLITICAL ACTORS OR CRIMINALS?

The strategic issue for the Colombian government is whether the self-defense groups should be treated as political actors—and therefore as legitimate participants in the peace negotiations—or as criminals to be suppressed. The AUC's near-term political objective is legitimacy and equal status with the guerrillas as political actors. Consequently, the AUC wants a seat at the table as a third party, although its leaders may actually have an interest in the continuation of the conflict, which perpetuates the conditions that permit the expansion of AUC influence.[21]

The Colombian government takes the view that the AUC is not a legitimate political organization and has excluded it from the negotiations. Although the Colombian government is committed to fighting the AUC as well as the guerrillas, the illegal self-defense groups are not seen by some sectors of Colombian public opinion as a strategic threat to the state in the same way that the guerrillas are.

From a pragmatic standpoint, whether the AUC is accepted as a legitimate political actor or not, it has become another competing power center challenging the state's frayed authority. Realistically, to the extent that these groups are the products of an environment of insecurity brought about by guerrilla activity and state weakness,

---

[19]"Colombian Death Squad Leader Reveals His Face," *CNN Interactive World Wide News*, March 2, 2000. See also Bagley, "The Evolution of Drug Trafficking in Colombia in the 1990s," pp. 9–10; and "The Andean Coca Wars: The Crop That Refuses to Die," *The Economist*, March 4, 2000.

[20]William Ledwith, Chief of the Drug Enforcement Agency's International Operations, before the House Government Reform Committee, Criminal Justice, Drug Policy and Human Resources Subcommittee, Washington, D.C., February 15, 2000.

[21]Rangel, p. 48.

they will continue to be a factor in Colombia's crisis as long as conditions are not changed.[22]

In view of these circumstances, it may be worth considering whether the policy of discouraging the organization of legal self-defense communities is wise. A network of supervised self-defense organizations on the Peruvian model could provide an alternative to the illegal groups. In the case of Peru, beginning with the administration of Alan García in the late 1980s and continuing under Fujimori, the Lima government organized and armed some 4000 *rondas campesinas*, or community self-defense militias. These militias played a decisive role in the defeat of the Peruvian insurgencies.[23] In the Colombian situation, a network of properly supervised self-defense organizations could give the state a better handle on the activities of self-organized local groups. Another alternative, suggested by military analyst David Spencer, is the establishment of National Guard units to provide local defense. To establish a National Guard organization, the Colombian military could draw on the pool of trained manpower created by the conscription system now in effect.[24] Whatever the modalities, such arrangements might help to create the conditions for a peace agreement by empowering local communities to provide for their security and creating incentives for the guerrillas to negotiate in good faith.

---

[22]At a conference in Washington, D.C., on September 27, 2000, it was the near-unanimous view of the Colombian mayors that it would be difficult to slow the growth of the illegal self-defense groups in the absence of an effective government presence at the local level.

[23]See Cynthia McClintock, "The Decimation of Peru's Sendero Luminoso," in Arnson.

[24]Personal communication from David Spencer, December 2000.

Chapter Six

COLOMBIAN GOVERNMENT STRATEGY

PLAN COLOMBIA

The Pastrana government's response to Colombia's crisis is Plan Colombia, a broad menu of proposals to deal with the economic, social, political, and military aspects of the situation.[1] Plan Colombia has ten elements:

- Economic recovery. The government sees free trade agreements and enhanced access to foreign markets to attract foreign and domestic investment as key to economic modernization and job creation.

- Fiscal and financial reform, including austerity and adjustment measures.

- A "peace strategy," with a view to achieving a negotiated peace settlement with the guerrillas.

- Strengthening the armed forces and the police so that they can restore the rule of law and security throughout the country.

- Judicial reform to reestablish the rule of law and ensure equal and impartial justice.

- A counter-narcotics strategy, in partnership with other countries. The centerpiece of this effort is the organizing and training of

---

[1] *Plan Colombia: Plan for Peace, Prosperity, and the Strengthening of the State*, Presidency of the Republic of Colombia, Bogotá, October 1999 edition.

new counter-narcotics battalions to be deployed to the coca-growing department of Putumayo (the "Drive to the South")[2]; the battalions' mission will be to secure the area while coca eradication takes place.

- Agricultural development and other economic activities to provide legal alternatives for coca farmers and coca plantation laborers.

- Popular mobilization to develop more accountability in local government, community involvement in anticorruption efforts, and pressure on the illegal armed groups to end kidnappings, violence, and the internal displacement of individuals and communities.

- Social programs, for health, education, and alleviation of poverty.

- Mobilization of the international community to participate in the Plan.

To underwrite the cost of Plan Colombia, the Pastrana government undertook to provide $4 billion in national funds, while seeking $3.5 billion in foreign assistance, largely from the United States, the European Union, Japan, Canada, and international financial institutions. Consistent with the U.S. policy focus on the drug problem in Colombia, 74 percent of U.S. assistance to Plan Colombia was earmarked to support counter-narcotics.[3] The Europeans, for their own part, prefer to channel their assistance to nonmilitary programs.

The U.S. Congress approved in July 2000 an emergency supplemental assistance request for fiscal years 2000–2001 of $1.32 billion, of which $862.3 million was allocated to Colombia and the balance to neighboring countries (primarily Peru, Bolivia, and Ecuador) and to U.S. agencies' Andean region antidrug operations. Of the $862.3 million allocated to Colombia, $521.2 million is new assistance to the Colombian armed forces and $123.1 million is assistance to the police, with the rest ($218 million) going to alternative eco-

---

[2]Colombia, Republic of. See also p. 64 ff.

[3]David Spencer and Heather Noss, p. 12.

nomic development, aid to displaced persons, judicial reform, law enforcement, and promotion of human rights.[4]

The bulk of the military assistance will support the Colombian armed forces' three counter-narcotics battalions, which are to receive 16 UH-60 Black Hawk and 30 UH-1H Huey transport helicopters. Police assistance goes to a variety of items, the largest of which is a grant of two Black Hawk and 12 Huey helicopters. The package includes $68.5 million for alternative economic development and crop substitution, including $10 million to assist farmers displaced by the anticipated coca eradication operations in southern Colombia. Some $51 million is provided to improve human rights protections, including the establishment of joint human rights units made up of prosecutors and judicial police, witness and judicial protection, and assistance to nongovernmental organizations and the UN High Commissioner for Human Rights' Bogotá field office.

The U.S. package comes with a number of conditions, including a requirement for certification regarding trials in civilian courts of military officers facing credible allegations of gross human rights violations, military cooperation with civilian investigators, vigorous prosecution in civilian courts of paramilitaries and military officers who aid or abet them, development of a Judge Advocate General corps in field units to investigate misconduct by military personnel, and development of a strategy to eliminate all coca and poppy production by 2005. There are also reporting requirements and a cap on U.S. military personnel or contractors in the country at any one time.[5] Members of the counter-narcotics units funded by U.S. assistance are individually screened for histories of human rights abuses.

There is a question of the practical limitations on the Colombian government's ability to prevent human rights violations in the context of an armed insurgency. The experience of other countries engaged in similar conflicts, including that of the United States in Vietnam, suggests that, even with disciplined troops, the chain of command will break down at times under the stress of armed conflict. That said, the Colombian government has made an effort to penalize

---

[4]For a description of the U.S. package, see Center for International Policy, "The Content of the Colombia Aid Package," www.ciponline.org/colombia/aid/aidsumm.htm.
[5]Ibid.

human rights violations by members of the armed and security forces. The investigation and prosecution of crimes by military personnel fall under the supervision of the Procurator General and is independent of the military chain of command. From 1997 to 1999, 477 members of the military and the police were tried and found guilty of human rights violations.[6]

While Plan Colombia was presented in the United States as a key component of a counter-narcotics strategy, it was presented in Europe as a means of furthering the peace negotiations and economic reconstruction.[7] Participants at a Plan Colombia donors' conference in Madrid in July 2000 agreed to provide an additional $619 million, mostly for social development projects. Spain was the largest donor, with a $100 million pledge. Japan and Norway pledged $70 million and $20 million, respectively. The rest of the funds were pledged by international financial institutions.[8] At a follow-up meeting in Bogotá in October 2000, representatives of the European Union agreed to contribute a total of $332 million (including the Spanish contribution) toward social and institutional development.[9]

COUNTER-NARCOTICS STRATEGY

The Colombian government's counter-narcotics strategy combines ongoing efforts to interdict the movement of illegal drugs and precursor chemicals, coca and poppy eradication, and destruction of drug-processing facilities, with a plan to retake control of the drug-producing areas. The first phase of the plan is to take control of the FARC-controlled coca-growing areas in the department of Putumayo in southern Colombia. Putumayo and the neighboring department of Caquetá account for over one half of Colombia's coca acreage.[10]

---

[6]República de Colombia, *La fuerza pública y los derechos humanos en Colombia,* pp. 24–25.

[7]Libardo González, "El Plan Colombia: una paz armada," Colombia Thema, No. 7, March–May 2000, http://www.colombia-thema.org.

[8]"La diplomacia saca la cara," *El Tiempo,* Bogotá, August 3, 2000.

[9]"Otros US$144 millones de Europa a Plan Colombia," *El Tiempo,* October 25, 2000.

[10]Putumayo accounts for 35,100 hectares of coca fields, and Caquetá for 28,000 hectares, out of a nationwide total of 122,500 hectares, according to figures provided in a Colombian armed forces briefing, April 2000. More recent estimates are higher.

In the second phase, counter-narcotics operations would extend to the coca-growing regions in southeastern and central Colombia, and finally, to the whole country. As noted above, the bulk of the U.S. assistance package is designed to help the Colombian government implement this "Southern strategy." Key priorities, as noted above, will be to train and equip the new counter-narcotics battalions. U.S. assistance also includes a program to improve the Colombian navy's control of traffic on the country's 18,000 kilometers of navigable rivers. A riverine brigade, with five battalions throughout the country, was established at Puerto Leguízamo, Putumayo, in August 1999. U.S. aid will also provide improved radar, airfields, and intelligence collection capabilities.

Although U.S. assistance is provided for counter-narcotics purposes only, there is a clear linkage between the Colombian government's counter-narcotics and counter-insurgency strategies. The Colombian government believes that, by striking at the drug trade, it also strikes at the economic center of gravity of the guerrillas. That is, by destroying the coca and poppy fields, drug-production facilities, and transportation networks, the government can also degrade the guerrillas' ability to carry on the war.[11]

Whether this is an accurate assessment remains to be seen. According to some Colombian analysts, the center of gravity of the guerrillas is not their links to the drug trade but their political control of small towns and rural areas.[12] Nevertheless, assuming that the government's strategy of reducing the cultivation, processing, and distribution of narcotics is correct and that the new counter-narcotics battalions can successfully execute it, there may still be a time lag between the execution of the strategy and its impact on FARC resources and capabilities. According to U.S. officials, the first Black Hawk helicopter may not arrive in Colombia until October 2002.[13] This period

---

According to Colombian officials, at the beginning of 2001 there were at least 138,000 acres (55,890 hectares) of coca fields in Putumayo. "Plan Colombia: Herbicide Sprayings Killing Food Crops," AP, January 23, 2001.

[11]Conversation with Colombian armed forces Commander General Tapias, Bogotá, April 2000.

[12]Discussion with Alfredo Rangel.

[13]Statement of Jess T. Ford, Director, International Affairs and Trade, U.S. General Accounting Office, before the U.S. House of Representatives, Subcommittee on Criminal

before the arrival of the U.S. military equipment may be the point of maximum danger for the Colombian government.

There is a broadly shared assumption in Colombia that the FARC will escalate its military attacks once the government's new counter-narcotics battalions begin to operate in southern Colombia, bringing about a conflation of the war on drugs and the political war. This could bring into relief the contradictions between the government's counter-narcotics and social and political objectives. According to the governor of Putumayo, about 135,000 of the department's 314,000 inhabitants depend directly on the coca crop for their liveli-hood.[14] Intensified coca eradication would probably be resisted by the local population, which would generate a serious social conflict, further delegitimize the Colombian government among the popu-lace, and strengthen support for the FARC.

There is already a great deal of criticism in Colombia of the govern-ment's policy of aerial spraying of coca and poppy fields. Critics note that the spraying has not prevented the tripling of the area under coca cultivation since Pastrana's inauguration, and that the spraying simply destroys the means of livelihood of subsistence farmers and displaces the crops deeper into the jungle.[15] The coca producers have also adapted by developing new varieties of the coca plant, such as the Tingo María, which produces three times as much coca as the traditional varieties.[16] The Colombian military is very much aware of the economic, social, and political consequences of counter-narcotics operations. In a discussion in Bogotá, General Tapias ex-plained the need for spraying—given the large extension of the areas under cultivation and the impracticality of other eradication meth-ods—but he also stressed that eradication alone would not work. It

Justice, Drug Policy, and Human Resources, Committee on Government Reform, October 12, 2000.

[14]Interview with Jorge Devia Murcia, governor of Putumayo, in *Colombia Update*, published by Colombia Human Rights Committee of Washington, D.C., Vol. 12, No. 1, Summer/Fall 2000, p. 7.

[15]Discussion with Horacio Serpa, former Colombian minister of interior, Washington, D.C., July 2000.

[16]Alfredo Molano, "Conflict, Peace, and International Intervention," *Colombia Up-date*, Vol. 12, No. 1, Summer/Fall 2000, p. 5.

would have to be accompanied by an effective economic development and employment-generation policy.[17]

ROLE OF THE UNITED STATES

For the Colombian government, the United States is the *deus ex machina* that would rescue it from its current predicament. The Pastrana government receives credit, even from political opponents, for having restored the cooperative relationship with the United States that had been badly frayed during the Samper presidency. At the same time, there has been criticism that the Colombian government strategy is driven by political constraints in U.S. policy that can justify aid to Colombia only in terms of counter-narcotics assistance.[18] This view is given further credence by the statement of a senior U.S. foreign policymaker at a U.S. Army War College Conference that the emphasis on counter-narcotics assistance represented a consensus within the U.S. government that could be placed at risk if the United States were to attempt to assume a counter-insurgency role.[19]

There has also been criticism of U.S. military support for the counter-narcotics aspect of Plan Colombia from some Colombians and Europeans on the grounds that it represents intensified militarization of the response to the drug problem and that it could undermine democracy and contribute to human rights abuses. Officials in Washington insist that they have little choice but to emphasize support for the Colombian military, given that the FARC and other illegal armed groups are involved in the drug trade.[20]

---

[17]Discussion with General Tapias.

[18]Discussion with Alfredo Rangel, Bogotá, Colombia, April 13, 2000. Colombian political scientist Francisco Leal Buitrago noted in a conversation with Dr. Rabasa that the first detailed draft of Plan Colombia was published, in English, right after U.S. Under Secretary of State Pickering's visit to Bogotá.

[19]Richard Downes, "Landpower and Ambiguous Warfare: The Challenge of Colombia in the 21st Century," U.S. Army War College, Strategic Studies Institute (SSI) Conference Report, March 10, 1999, p. 13.

[20]Discussion with Bruce Bagley, University of Miami, February 11, 2000. See also Zirnite, p. 166.

The FARC clearly believes that U.S. counter-narcotics assistance is directed against it, that it is, in effect, disguised counter-insurgency assistance, and that if they, the guerrillas, were to gain the upper hand, the United States would intervene on the side of the Bogotá government. Therefore, in its public posture, the FARC has stressed the threat that U.S. military assistance to Colombia poses to the peace process, a theme that plays well with some domestic and international audiences. The FARC professes to be opposed in principle to the narcotics trade, while criticizing the methods employed by the Colombian government—aerial spraying in particular. It has also sought to forestall direct U.S. intervention by drawing parallels between Colombia and Vietnam.

Colombia's neighbors are caught between a hammer and an anvil. On the one hand, with the possible exception of Venezuela, they formally support Plan Colombia. As the Ecuadorean Foreign Minister stated in Washington in October 2000, Colombia's neighbors understand that the Colombian drug-producing and drug-trafficking complex is a cancer that needs to be extirpated. On the other hand, they fear that if the attack on drugs in Putumayo is successful, it might succeed in driving the drug problem across the border into their countries (see Chapter Nine).

The core question for policymakers is: Will the U.S. assistance program as currently structured help the Colombian government reduce the threats of drugs and insurgency and restore its authority? This question can be subdivided into a number of issues. Strategic and operational issues are discussed in Chapter Ten. Two questions are discussed here: Is the level of U.S. assistance adequate? Can it be sustained? The view of many Colombian and U.S. experts is that the current level of U.S. assistance is insufficient to alter the balance of forces. Participants at a symposium sponsored by the Center for Naval Analyses (CNA) in October 2000 noted that the Colombian fleet of helicopters and fixed-wing aircraft is roughly the same size as that of the Salvadoran military at the peak of the war in El Salvador, which was fought on a territory one fiftieth the size of Colombia.[21] A U.S. General Accounting Office (GAO) official stated in congressional testimony in October 2000 that U.S. officials believe that substantial

---

[21]Spencer and Noss, p. 8.

funding for Plan Colombia beyond that planned for fiscal years 2000–2001 would be needed. In addition to the issue of overall assistance levels, the GAO has questioned whether the United States has provided adequate spare parts and funding to maintain and operate helicopters provided under the counter-narcotics assistance program.[22]

Will the United States provide sustained, high levels of assistance? The United States has committed to underwrite support for the counter-narcotics efforts in Colombia for the next two years (fiscal years 2000–2001). The Colombian government's stated goal is to eliminate all coca and poppy production by 2005. From December 2000 to February 2001, U.S.-backed antidrug drives resulted in the destruction of more than 29,000 hectares of coca fields (enough to produce 200–250 tons of cocaine annually). However, there are serious questions as to whether this rate of coca eradication can be sustained. Many areas still to be targeted are harder to reach and under FARC control.[23] Indeed, most experts, including some U.S. officials, agree that the type of response that is currently being emphasized by Washington would require a sustained level of commitment over a long period of time.[24] Certainly, to expect Colombia to take up the slack should the level of U.S. assistance drop substantially after fiscal year 2001 is unrealistic, particularly given the country's economic difficulties[25] and the technical challenges of maintaining advanced military equipment.

The implications of the U.S. assistance program for Colombia are that the United States, by taking the lead in mustering international support for Plan Colombia, has increased its political stake in Colombia. If the Pastrana administration falters, either in its counter-narcotics or counter-insurgency approach, the United States would be confronted with an unpalatable choice. It could escalate its commitment, to include perhaps an operational role for U.S. forces in Colombia, or scale it down, which could involve

---

[22]Statement of Jess T. Ford, fn 13.

[23]*Financial Times*, February 20, 2001.

[24]Bagley. See also "U.S. Officials Say Anti-Drug Plan for Colombia Will Take Time to Show Results," CNN Interactive World Wide News, February 22, 2000; Ford testimony, fn 13.

[25]Shifter, "The United States and Colombia: Partners in Ambiguity," p. 53.

some significant costs, including a serious loss of credibility and degradation of the U.S. ability to muster regional support for its counter-narcotics and political objectives. At the same time, Bogotá has essentially adopted a U.S. vision of the problem—which focuses on narcotics eradication—as the centerpiece of its strategy. As a result, it has gained access to substantial U.S. resources, but at the cost of a loss of flexibility to design and implement its own solutions.

Chapter Seven

THE PEACE NEGOTIATIONS

The Pastrana government's hopes for restoring peace rest in the success of negotiations with the guerrillas. This is not a new approach. Periodic truces, cease-fires, and attempts to reach a negotiated settlement have punctuated the 35-year Colombian insurgency. The administration of President Belisario Betancur, a populist Conservative, signed a ten-month truce with the M-19 revolutionary movement in August 1984; however, the M-19 broke off the talks and in November 1985 an M-19 commando group seized the Palace of Justice in central Bogotá. Over 100 people were killed in the ensuing battle, including 11 Supreme Court justices. A truce with the FARC and parts of the ELN was in effect from 1984 to 1987. The FARC established a political front, the Patriotic Union (UP), which contested the 1986 election and elected 14 senators and congressmen and scores of council members. However, the agreement unraveled amid mutual recriminations and assassinations of UP officials; it was broken off by the government after a FARC ambush of an army unit in Caquetá.[1]

Unlike Betancur, who had avoided the issue of disarmament in negotiations with the guerrillas, his successor, Liberal President Virgilio Barco (1986–1990), insisted that the negotiations be limited to two fundamental issues: disarmament of the guerrillas and their reincorporation into society. Barco's approach achieved a major success in 1989 when the M-19 broke ranks with other guerrilla groups and

---

[1]See Mark Chernick, "Negotiating Peace Amid Multiple Forms of Violence," in Arnson, pp. 175–177; and "De Caracas al Caguán," *Cambio*, Bogotá, July 3–10, 2000.

agreed to abandon the armed struggle in exchange for amnesty and guarantees of participation in the political process. The M-19 participated in the 1990 presidential and parliamentary elections; it received almost 30 percent of the vote in a special election for a Constituent Assembly, and its leader, Antonio Navarro Wolff, became one of three co-presidents of the assembly, as well as a member of President César Gaviria's cabinet.[2]

The Gaviria administration (1990–1994) followed the Barco model in its successful negotiations with several small guerrilla groups: the People's Liberation Army (EPL), the Quintín Lame group, and the Revolutionary Workers' Party (PRT), all of which laid down their arms and were given representation in the Constituent Assembly. Next, the government entered into negotiations with the FARC and the ELN, which had joined other guerrilla groups in the Simón Bolívar Guerrilla Coordinator (CGSB). The CGSB demanded a broader agenda than disarmament and reincorporation and insisted on maintaining its forces in the areas where it had major influence. The government and the CGSB met in Caracas, Venezuela, but the negotiations were suspended after a FARC ambush of the president of the senate's motorcade in September 1991. The discussions were resumed in Tlaxcala, Mexico, in March 1992, but were again suspended after the dissident faction of the EPL, a participant in the guerrilla coalition, kidnapped and killed a former government minister.[3]

Gaviria's successor, Liberal President Ernesto Samper (1994–1998), sought a resumption of peace negotiations through a National Conciliation Commission. The guerrillas, branded as bandits by the Gaviria government after the end of the Tlaxcala talks, were once again relegitimized as negotiating partners. The government, the ELN, and representatives of civil society sectors agreed to discuss the application of international humanitarian norms to the conflict, but

---

[2]Chernick, pp. 178–180. Despite its impressive initial display of electoral strength, the M-19 failed to establish itself as a political force and saw its political fortunes decline precipitously in subsequent elections.

[3]Chernick, pp. 180–183; "De Caracas al Caguán"; for the FARC perspective see Fuerzas Armadas, Revolucionarias de Colombia, "Las FARC: 30 años de lucha por la paz, democracia y soberanía, http://tierra.ucsd.edu/farc-ep/Nuestra_historia. As noted above, the main body of the EPL agreed to demobilize in the context of a peace agreement in 1990.

the FARC demanded the demilitarization of an area in southern Colombia as a precondition for negotiations. Discussions with other guerrilla groups produced limited results.[4]

Andrés Pastrana, a coalition presidential candidate supported by the Conservative Party and dissident Liberals and independents, was elected president in July 1998 on a platform of peace negotiations. In November 1998, President Pastrana withdrew government forces from five municipalities in southern Colombia. Talks began in the town of San Vicente del Cagúan, within the *zona de despeje*, or demilitarized zone, in January 1999. Pastrana traveled to the zone to open the negotiations, but was snubbed by FARC leader Marulanda, who failed to appear (supposedly on security grounds). The FARC then suspended the negotiations, 18 days after they had started, demanding that Pastrana curb the paramilitary groups' activities. The ELN, in turn, demanded equal treatment with the FARC and in April 1999 hijacked an airplane to press its demands.[5]

Negotiations with the FARC resumed in May 1999. The negotiations were, in a sense, a continuation of those of 1991–1992 in that the stated objectives of the two sides had not changed much over the intervening years. The government continued to seek the demobilization of the guerrilla forces, while the guerrillas wanted to discuss a broad-ranging social, economic, and political agenda and defer the issues of demobilization and security guarantees. What had changed was the correlation of forces. In the intervening years, the FARC had expanded its military strength and zone of influence. While in 1991–1992 the guerrillas agreed to negotiate at venues overseas, in 1998 they insisted that the negotiations take place in zones cleared of government forces and effectively controlled by the guerrillas.

Negotiations between the Pastrana government and the FARC continued, with periodic interruptions, through 1999 and 2000, without registering any perceptible results. They were broken off by the FARC in November 2000 to protest the alleged government failure to combat the illegal self-defense (paramilitary) groups. The stalled negotiations were dealt another blow in December 2000,

---

[4]Chernick, pp. 183–185. See chronology in Echandía, pp. 217–223.

[5]"Colombia: desintegración o intervención en ciernes?" *Venezuela Analítica*, September 9, 1999.

when FARC guerrillas ambushed and executed Diego Turbay, the head of the congressional peace commission, and five others, including his mother, in southern Caquetá.[6] The talks resumed in February 2001 after the government threatened to move against the *zone de despeje*. The agenda for the renewed negotiations included a ceasefire, a prisoner exchange, and the creation of a commission to find ways to combat the paramilitary groups and ameliorate the effects of the conflict. The FARC also announced that it was not opposed to the eradication of coca crops, as long as there were economic alternatives.[7]

As of this writing, the negotiations had involved only the FARC, although the government had opened discussions with the ELN with a view to beginning parallel negotiations. The ELN's central demand is to be given control of a zone analogous to that conceded to the FARC. The Pastrana administration has agreed in principle to what it calls a *zona de convivencia* (live-and-let-live zone) for the ELN in an area in the middle Magdalena valley, where it has long been active. However, chastened by the FARC's exploitation of the *zona de despeje* in southern Colombia, the government proposes to make the ELN zone smaller (about 5000 square kilometers) and include safeguards in the arrangement, such as the continued operations of the civil authorities within the zone and a "security cordon" around it to prevent it from becoming another sanctuary for illegal activities.[8]

PROSPECTS FOR A PEACE SETTLEMENT

Do the conditions exist for the successful conclusion of a peace agreement? There is little question about the Colombian government's commitment to achieving a negotiated settlement. A debate within the Pastrana administration on the extent of the concessions

---

[6]Turbay was traveling in an armored vehicle to the town of Puerto Rico to attend the swearing-in of the new mayor.

[7]"Segundo Aire," *Cambio*, February 12–19, 2000.

[8]"Proceso con ELN, aún sin definiciones," *El Tiempo*, December 24, 1999; Daniel García Peña, "The National Liberation Army (ELN) Creates a Different Peace Process," Colombia Report, November 27, 2000, www.colombiareport.org/colombia41.html; "Los acuerdos de la Habana," *Cambio*, January 22–29, 2001.

to be made to the FARC was settled within the first year of the administration with the resignation of Defense Minister Rodrigo Lloreda in May 1999. Backed by the military high command, Lloreda opposed Pastrana's decision to extend indefinitely the *zona de despeje*. The government's agreement to the FARC's negotiating agenda and its refusal to enter into discussions with the illegal self-defense forces constituted significant concessions.

What is in question is whether there are sufficient incentives for the guerrillas—primarily the FARC—to make peace now. There are three keys to this question: the first is the long-term political objectives of the guerrillas. The second is the evolution of the political-military situation or, more accurately, the guerrillas' perception of it, including its international aspects. The third is the role of the illegal self-defense forces.

There is controversy regarding the true nature of the FARC and its objectives. One view is that the FARC is no longer pursuing its original goal of Marxist revolution and is more interested in the limited goal of empowering the historically disenfranchised Colombian peasantry. Another view, commonly held in counter-narcotics circles, is that the guerrillas have become nothing more than drug traffickers and that their motivations are undistinguishable from those of common criminals. Neither view is consistent with the FARC's behavior as a revolutionary political organization and its continued adherence to its stated goal of toppling the Colombian government.[9] The ELN may be another matter. The ELN suffered some heavy blows, particularly at the hands of paramilitary groups and, according to an interlocutor familiar with the thinking of ELN leaders, might be willing to settle for less than a full share of power.

It is worth noting, as one perceptive analyst of the Colombian conflict, Alfredo Rangel, has pointed out, that the guerrillas and the

---

[9]Colombian analysts differ on the question of the FARC's willingness to negotiate a peace agreement, but most reject the view that its members have become "narco-guerrillas" or simply a new cartel. García-Peña argues that it is precisely because of their strongly held ideological convictions that the guerrillas require funding to finance their growth and operations. In other words, guerrilla wealth is not an end in itself, but a means to an end. Daniel García-Peña, "The Colombian Peace Process," in James L. Zackrison (ed.), *Crisis: What Crisis? Security Issues in Colombia*, INSS, National Defense University, Washington, D.C., 1999, p. 58.

government operate with different conceptions of time, and that these conceptions shape their respective approaches to the negotiations. Having fought for 35 years in the mountains of Colombia, the FARC leaders can afford to be patient. They believe, moreover, that time is on their side, and that with the passage of time the FARC strengthens its position, gains legitimacy, and increases its resources and its influence. The Colombian government, in contrast, is constrained by the electoral schedule and its need to meet the electorate's expectations, as well as by external pressures and deadlines. The Pastrana government has until the next presidential election in 2002 to achieve its objective of a peace settlement. From these differing conceptions of the time element derive the Pastrana government's desire to press on with the negotiations and the FARC's dilatory tactics.[10]

The second factor is the evolution of the politico-military situation. Even if the FARC leaders are orthodox Marxists whose long-term goal is the seizure of power, they are not "fundamentalists," in the view of a respected Colombian analyst. Rather, they are *campesinos sensatos,* shrewd peasants perfectly capable of rational calculations.[11] As long as they believe that military trends are running in their favor and that they may be able to win a military victory, or at least dictate the terms of the peace, the FARC will have little incentive to settle. On the other hand, if the FARC becomes convinced that a military victory is not possible, it might accept a negotiated end to the conflict.

The third factor is the illegal self-defense forces, which present a dilemma for all the other parties. The government, for good reasons, including the AUC's responsibility for some of the most egregious human rights violations, wishes to deny them the legitimacy that they would acquire from participation in the negotiations. The guerrillas have insisted on their exclusion, but at the same time they argue that, for their own safety, they cannot demobilize as long as the

[10]Rangel, pp. 8–9.

[11]Discussion with Francisco Leal Buitrago, Bogotá, April 2000. Based on his analysis of FARC documents and interviews with FARC guerrillas, Spencer takes the view that the FARC leaders are not *campesinos sensatos,* but fundamentalists. Personal communication, December 2000.

paramilitaries are not also demobilized. But the AUC, which is not a party to the negotiations, has no incentive to demobilize.

With these caveats, the successful peace settlements in El Salvador and Guatemala may provide lessons for Colombia. In El Salvador, direct contacts between the government and the representatives of the guerrillas began in 1984, after the military situation had developed into a stalemate and the United States had made clear that it would not permit the military defeat of the Salvadoran government. The peace accords, concluded in January 1992, created a human rights ombudsman, established a separate National Civil Police to safeguard public security, formerly the responsibility of the armed forces, and permitted the major guerrilla umbrella organization, the Farabundo Martí National Liberation Front (FMLN) to transform itself into a legal political party.[12]

In Guatemala, the government opened direct negotiations with an essentially defeated guerrilla coalition, the Unidad Revolucionaria Nacional Guatemalteca (URNG) in 1991. The negotiations lasted five years and covered an agenda containing 11 themes divided into two groups: substantive issues related to deep-seated problems, and operational issues, including the demobilization of the guerrillas and their reincorporation into the political process. In both cases, despite initial distrust, the armed forces understood and supported the peace process.[13]

In Colombia, the guerrillas have not been defeated (unlike Guatemala), and the dynamic military situation cannot be considered a stalemate (unlike El Salvador). In both the Salvadoran and Guatemalan cases, as well as other successful peace processes, the key factor in reaching a settlement was the agreement of the rebel forces to demobilize in exchange for their incorporation into a democratic political process. In Colombia, the guerrillas have not shown any willingness to give up their arms as part of a peace agreement and no viable solution has been suggested to the problem of the paramilitaries.

---

[12]See Brigadier General Nelson Ivan Saldaña Araújo, "The Process of Negotiations in El Salvador," in Zackrison (ed.), pp. 45–47.

[13]Brigadier General Otto Molina, "The Peace Process in Guatemala," in Zackrison (ed.), pp. 39–43.

Yet, while it may not be in the FARC's interest to reach a settlement at this time, neither does it want the negotiations to break down irretrievably. Both the government and the FARC have an interest in continuing the process, regardless of how dim the prospects for success might be. The government has staked its credibility on the negotiations track and hopes that the negotiations will develop a momentum that will enmesh the guerrillas in the process. For the FARC, the negotiating arrangements enhance its domestic and international stature and legitimacy and create real strategic and operational advantages—particularly the ability to operate freely in the *zona de despeje.*

CONCLUSIONS

Given these considerations, it is unlikely that the peace negotiations will drive the political process in Colombia in the near term. The dynamic element driving the prospects of real peace will be evolution of the balance of forces. The position of the sides in the negotiations will no doubt reflect this evolving balance. Both sides will likely try to use the negotiations for tactical purposes as an element in their larger political and information warfare strategies (although the FARC has been much more adept than the government at this).

A critical point will come with the prospective deployment of the government's new counter-narcotics brigade to the south. The FARC has tried to use the negotiations to forestall the deployment and will probably intensify these efforts as the time comes nearer. If the FARC is not successful in deterring the deployment, it would be confronted with a choice of breaking off the negotiations, as it has threatened to do if the Colombian government proceeds with its deployment plans, or acquiescing, and thereby suffering a clear political defeat. The FARC could also choose to preempt the government's deployment and go on the offensive.

Chapter Eight

COLOMBIAN FUTURES

What future will emerge from the collision of Colombian government and guerrilla strategies? There are several alternate scenarios for Colombia (although we recognize that the country could move sequentially through one or more of these on its trajectory to what ultimately might be a more stable state). We will describe each in turn, and in the process try to answer some of the key questions about the intentions, capabilities, and calculations of the main actors in this drama.

SCENARIO 1: SUCCESSFUL PEACE AGREEMENT

A peace agreement, if reached, could take one of two basic forms. The Central American model involves the negotiation of arrangements that provide for the end of the armed conflicts, the incorporation of former insurgents into the political process, and the adjudication of issues of governance through competitive elections. In the case of El Salvador, the transition from civil war to peace and reconciliation went through two stages. The first stage involved the implementation of the basic elements in the peace accords, with international verification. The FMLN guerrillas agreed to lay down their arms and demobilize. The Salvadoran armed forces were reduced in size and restructured, with their role limited to external defense. The records of military officers were reviewed by an ad hoc commission so that those responsible for human rights violations would be discharged or transferred. The security forces—National Police, Treasury Police, and National Guard—were disbanded and replaced with a National Civil Police. The second stage involved the consolidation of democratic norms, institutions, and practices. A Truth Commission was established to bring to light the truth about acts of violence in the preceding decade. New institutions, such as the Office of the Human Rights Ombudsman (*Procuraduría para la Defense de los Derechos Humanos*), were established to ensure public security and respect for human rights.[1]

An agreement based on this model is the preferred outcome for the Pastrana administration and the majority of Colombians. However, as discussed in the preceding chapter, there has been little or no progress on the fundamental issues of demobilization and development of a political framework that would permit the incorporation of the guerrillas into normal politics.

A variation of a peace agreement would fall short of the Central American standard of demobilization and political restructuring. In this variation, the two sides could agree on what amounts to a ceasefire—and perhaps a partial demobilization of the guerrillas, but with the guerrillas retaining control of areas where they are currently dominant. A reported Colombian government plan in 1991 contemplated the establishment of some 60 "mini-demilitarized zones" throughout the country as part of a peace settlement.[2] This scenario could move the country in either of two directions. In the best (but unlikely) case, it could be a transitional stage on the way to a comprehensive peace agreement. Conversely, it could lead to a fragmentation scenario by sanctioning a de facto partition of Colombia into government-controlled and guerrilla-controlled areas.[3]

SCENARIO 2: TURNING THE TIDE

In this scenario, the government gains the upper hand. The Colombian government and military get a handle on the political-military situation and begin to gain the upper hand in the struggle against the

---

[1]See Arnson, pp. 70–95, 394–396.

[2]"Los últimos estrenos, sin hacer cola," *Cambio*, July 3–10, 2000.

[3]A peace scenario would also require the participation or acquiescence of the illegal self-defense forces, given that the guerrillas are unlikely to agree to demobilize without parallel demobilization by other armed groups.

guerrillas and other illegal armed groups. This scenario assumes that the Colombian army is able to seize the strategic and operational initiative from the guerrillas and establish effective area control. (See Chapter Ten for details on Colombian military requirements.) Turning the tide may require retaking the FARC-controlled "demilitarized zone" in order to deprive the guerrillas of sanctuaries and to disrupt their infrastructure—particularly the critical logistics and troop mobility corridors.

If this scenario were to develop, it could create the conditions for a peace agreement. The guerrillas would realize that the war cannot be won and that continuing on that path would lead to defeat. This could lead to a "Guatemalan" or "Salvadoran" solution.

On the other hand, if the guerrillas came to the realization that their ability to influence the outcome of the war was waning, they might be driven to an all-out military effort, possibly calibrated to have the maximum psychological impact on the Colombian government and people and Colombia's international supporters. This effort could involve such spectacular actions as an attack on Bogotá and other major cities (the "Tet offensive" option); an attempt to take the Colombian government forward base at Tres Esquinas in Putumayo, the prospective base for the army's new counter-narcotics battalions (the "Khe Sanh" option); or an ambush of one of the counter-narcotics battalions in FARC-dominated territory in southern Colombia.

SCENARIO 3: STALEMATE

Neither the government nor the guerrillas can attain a military victory over the other. This scenario is viewed as the most plausible by some observers. As in the case of El Salvador, a stalemate could continue for a prolonged period. However, a stalemate may not prove to be a stable condition, and over time the balance will likely shift to one side or the other. The shift, if it occurs, could be rapid and lead to a sudden collapse of one of the sides (cf. China in 1949, Cuba in 1959, and Nicaragua in 1979).

SCENARIO 4: THE PERUVIAN MODEL

In this scenario—the *fujimorazo* in the Colombian vernacular—desperate Colombians look to former Peruvian President Fujimori's defeat of the Shining Path insurgency in the early 1990s as a model for Colombia. The Peruvian model would involve breaking negotiations and unleashing the full force of the state's military and security apparatus against the guerrillas. A decision to wage all-out war against the guerrillas would probably lower any priority on legal rights and introduce such practices as trials of suspected guerrillas or collaborators by secret military courts. It would also imply a decision by the Colombian government to "go it alone," because the United States and European donors could react by curtailing aid. This scenario would become more likely in the event of continued deterioration and loss of confidence by the Colombian people in the current strategy. As in the case of Peru, it could be initiated by government leaders themselves, with the support of the military, or by the military, with the support of political leaders (as in the 1953 military coup that brought to power Colombia's only military government in the 20th century).

SCENARIO 5: DISINTEGRATION

Deterioration continues and the war degenerates into an all-out struggle between the self-defense forces and the FARC. The government is unable to cope with the escalating violence and withdraws to the capital and some of the major cities. Government at the local level is coopted by armed groups, as has already occurred to some degree in many areas. Autonomous power centers emerge where local military commanders assume political leadership roles and join forces with self-defense groups. The situation could resemble Mexico after the 1910 Revolution, with regionally based armies vying for control of the symbols of central authority.

SCENARIO 6: FARC TAKEOVER OR POWER-SHARING

Deterioration continues, leading to a takeover by the FARC or to a peace agreement heavily tilted toward the FARC. In the first variation, the FARC could establish a state that will likely replicate Cuban characteristics, including a centralized authoritarian political system, dissolution of the armed forces and the political structures of the old regime, nationalization of large sectors of the economy and controls on economic activity, an "anti-imperialist" foreign policy, and the exodus of much of the Colombian middle class. The second variation could involve a peace agreement heavily tilted toward the FARC. It could include a coalition government acceptable to the FARC, a power-sharing arrangement that leaves the FARC in charge of large parts of Colombia (including the coca-growing regions), and the removal of U.S. influence.

SCENARIO 7: INTERNATIONALIZATION OF THE CONFLICT

As noted earlier, the armed conflict in Colombia has already spilled over to its neighbors. In this scenario, a FARC victory (or impending victory) could impel neighboring states to seek multilateral intervention, possibly under the umbrella of the Organization of American States (as in the Dominican Republic in 1964). The incentive for this course of action would be great if there appeared to be a possibility of the restoration of the Colombian government. If threatened by outside intervention, the FARC could seek to attack targets outside of Colombia, such as the Panama Canal locks, and step up support of other Latin American radical groups. Such a development would likely reenergize radical movements and armed insurgencies from Peru to Mexico that have been defused or contained over the past decade. The worst-case variation would be an alliance of a FARC government in Colombia with a radicalized government in Venezuela and the destabilization of Ecuador and Peru, leading to the emergence of a belt of radical states across northern and western South America.

PROBABLE FUTURE PATH

The interaction of the trend lines described in the preceding chapters will determine which of these Colombian futures ocurs. Although the direction of the trends is not positive, the deterioration of the Colombian government's position has not reached an irreversible stage. Currently there is a stalemate, with all sides preparing for an intensified level of violence. The catalyst is expected to be the government's implementation of the "Drive to the South" anticipated in Plan Colombia. Alternatively, the FARC could decide to preempt the government's advance in Putumayo by escalating the war in other parts of Colombia. This new phase of the war could witness the use of surface-to-air missiles by the guerrillas to deny the government use of helicopters and aircraft or inflict a major defeat on one of the new counter-narcotics battalions. Escalation of the fighting will likely be accompanied by mobilization of the civilian population in the guerrilla-controlled areas to oppose government counter-narcotics operations. Through its international support network, the FARC can also be expected to seek to deny international assistance to the Colombian government.

As noted earlier, a stalemate is not likely to be stable at an intensified level of violence, and over time the balance will tilt to one side or the other. The Colombian government, left to its own devices, does not have the institutional or material resources to reverse unfavorable trends, but the FARC also has weaknesses that could be exploited. The FARC's political weakness—lack of support among the population at large—raises the possibility that the guerrilla threat could be contained or defeated if the government succeeds in enlisting active popular support and seizing the strategic and operational initiative.

U.S. assistance to the Colombian government and armed forces in developing an effective strategy and acquiring the capabilities to implement it will be an important factor influencing Colombia's path. That factor, together with Bogotá's receptivity to innovation in its politico-military approach, will have a major influence on whether the Colombian government is able to turn the tide or whether deterioration continues, leading to one of the downside scenarios described above.

In any intensified conflict scenario—regardless of which side holds the advantage—the regional effects of the Colombian situation are likely to become amplified. The next chapter analyzes the effect of the Colombian conflict on neighboring states and the prospects that it will metastasize into a wider regional upheaval.

Chapter Nine

A WIDER CONFLICT?

There has already been a significant spillover of the armed conflict in Colombia. The contraction of the Colombian government's authority has facilitated the spread of guerrilla, paramilitary, and drug trafficking activities to neighboring states.

PANAMA

With highly permeable land, sea, and air borders with Colombia, a well-developed financial and commercial infrastructure (including the Colón Free Zone, the second largest in the world), and negligible security forces, Panama has become a critical node in the Colombian narcotraffickers' and guerrillas' support structure. Drugs transit Panama from Colombia for transshipment to the United States and Europe, while arms and supplies move the other way. Outside of major towns, the Panamanian authorities have lost control of the southernmost province of Darién, bordering on Colombia, which has effectively become an extension of the Colombian northwestern theater of operations. According to Panamanian sources, two battalion-sized FARC fronts, the 57th and 58th, operate in Darién, and the FARC maintains a major logistics and support base in Panamanian territory near the Colombian border. The narcotraffickers and guerrillas have also developed a support infrastructure in small ports on the Atlantic coast of Panama that enables them to move drugs, arms, supplies, and personnel by sea.

Panamanian security forces—a national police force that includes a specialized component with rudimentary light infantry training, and air and naval services—are no match for the heavily armed Colombian guerrillas. Panamanian strategy is to maintain a presence in the main towns in Darién province to provide static protection to the population, but without attempting to control the border (an impossible task in any event, given the difficulties of the terrain) or to confront the guerrillas that operate on the Panamanian side of the border.

The Panamanian air service is composed of a squadron of light transport aircraft (Casa 212s, BN2 Islanders), a squadron of UH-1H helicopters donated by the United States and Taiwan, and a training squadron (Chilean T-35s). The air service can operate only in daytime and below a ceiling of 10,000 feet. It has no close air support, air monitoring, or air interception capabilities. The air service is outclassed by the opposition, which employs higher-speed fixed-wing aircraft (ranging from Lear jets to Cessna 172s) and helicopters with extended range.[1]

The Panamanian naval force relies mostly on 63-ft to 105-ft patrol boats (donated by the United States) with average speeds of 15 knots and some captured fast boats. As in the case of the air service, the naval force's boats are no match for the fast boats used by Colombian narcotraffickers and guerrillas, which are capable of speeds of up to 50 knots and have greater maneuverability and shallow-water capabilities.

U.S. and Panamanian observers agree that the Panamanian security forces would not be able to protect the Canal—or Panamanian sovereignty over large swaths of its territory—if the Colombian guerrillas launched a determined attack. The constraints on a guerrilla move against Panama or the Canal are largely political: first, the current arrangement works for the guerrillas and they have no apparent incentive to overturn it. Second, the Panama Canal is now controlled by Panama and an attack on the Canal would be considered an attack on Panama rather than on the United States; third, the main users of the Canal are South American countries, which would be the most severely affected by its closure. However, a change in the situation in Colombia—for instance, if the Colombian government succeeded in putting real pressure on the guerrillas—could

---

[1]Reportedly, these helicopters can be flown without refueling from Colombia to Guatemala, roughly the distance from Washington, D.C., to Miami.

change the guerrillas' calculations. In that scenario, the FARC could move into Panama in a major way and threaten the Canal and other strategic U.S. interests.[2]

VENEZUELA

Venezuela is a critical country for U.S. and Colombian security interests. Not only is Venezuela one of the world's largest oil producers—with proved reserves of 73 billion barrels of oil and as much as 1.3 trillion barrels of extra-heavy oil, including bitumen—it is an important regional actor whose international and domestic policies can have a significant and possibly decisive impact on the conflict in Colombia. From their own perspective, Venezuelans believe that, as a neighbor with a long, guerrilla-infested border with Colombia, their security is directly bound with that of Colombia. The Venezuelans are also concerned about the large-scale illegal migration of Colombians to Venezuela and the development of transborder links between criminal networks in both countries.

About one third of the Venezuelan armed forces are deployed on the border with Colombia in an effort to seal the border against undesirable elements. Venezuelans complain that the Colombians are not doing enough to control their side of the border,[3] although the Colombians point out that they have insufficient forces to control the border and fight the insurgency. The Venezuelan armed forces are actively engaged in antinarcotics operations, but there are indications that they have adopted an avoidance strategy toward the guerrillas. Complicating this picture is Venezuela's political revolution, which brought to power Hugo Chávez—a former Army officer and a leader of a 1992 coup attempt. Chávez' authoritarian tendencies and links to Fidel Castro and the Colombian guerrillas have raised concerns about the direction of his government and the future of democracy in Venezuela, straining relations with the United States.[4]

---

[2]The sources of this review of Panama's role in the Colombian crisis are discussions with Panamanian national police, air service, and naval service senior leaders and Panamanian political leaders and security analysts, Panama City, April 2000.

[3] Discussion with senior Venezuelan military officers, Caracas, April 2000.

[4]Chávez has taken steps to distance the Venezuelan armed forces from the U.S. military. He has forbidden overflights of Venezuelan territory by U.S. aircraft on regional

Chávez has sought to play an active role in the diplomacy of the Colombian conflict, but his initiatives are viewed with suspicion by Colombians, who question his motives and accuse him of intervening inappropriately in domestic Colombian affairs. There is no evidence that the Chávez government is giving material support to the Colombian guerrillas, but weapons captured from guerrillas in 2000 turned out to have come from Venezuelan army stocks, leading to a protest by the Colombian authorities.[5]   In November 2000, the Colombian press reported that the ELN operates an office in Caracas and ELN representatives meet regularly with Chávez and his inner circle. According to the same reports, a high-level Venezuelan military officer met clandestinely with FARC leader Marulanda in FARC-controlled territory in Colombia to arrange for the release of Venezuelan cattlemen held by the FARC and negotiate a non-aggression agreement.[6]

The United States, therefore, cannot assume that Venezuela will cooperate in efforts to strengthen the Colombian government vis-à-vis the guerrillas. However, Chávez' relationship with the Colombian guerrillas is a double-edged sword. He may be able to provide political support for the guerrillas, perhaps in the guise of peacemaking, but overt support could generate a hostile regional and international reaction and perhaps undermine his position at home, particularly with the private sector and the military.

ECUADOR

In unstable Ecuador, already the victim of cross-border raids from Colombia, there is fear that the Colombian guerrillas and drug traffickers could move in force across the border and perhaps join forces with local dissidents. Pro-FARC mayors have taken office in some of the northern Ecuadorean cities, including the provincial capital of Lago Agrio. A group named the Revolutionary Armed Forces of

---

antinarcotics missions; ordered its navy not to participate in the multinational 2000 UNITA exercise, the first time in 42 years that Venezuela did not take part; and ordered its air force to pull out of Red Flag, only one or two days before the exercise was to begin.

[5]"El silencio sobre las armas," *Venezuela Analítica*, July 24, 2000.

[6]"La mano de Chávez," *Cambio*, November 21, 2000.

Ecuador has launched a propaganda campaign against Plan Colombia in northern Ecuador.[7] The 29th, 32nd, and 48th FARC fronts operate in Nariño and Putumayo, Colombian departments bordering on Ecuador, and Ecuadorean troops and suspected Colombian guerrillas have clashed well within the territory of Ecuador.[8]

In response, Ecuador has increased its presence on the border with Colombia[9] and plans to increase development spending by $300 million over the next four years in the bordering provinces. The Ecuadorean government plan is to create a social and economic "buffer zone" and prevent the spread of coca cultivation to the Ecuadorean side of the border. The Ecuadoreans are also concerned about the influx of refugees. At an October 23, 2000, press conference in Washington, Ecuadorean Foreign Minister Heinz Moeller stated that Ecuador recognizes its international obligation to accept refugees, but wants mechanisms to ensure the return of refugees to Colombia and that the refugee camps do not become bases of operations for drug traffickers and guerrillas.[10]

Ecuadorean authorities coordinate with the Colombian government regarding the common threat from guerillas and narcotraffickers. In August 2000, the new Ecuadorean president, Gustavo Noboa, traveled to Bogotá to ask President Pastrana to keep the Quito government informed of military operations in southern Colombia so that the Ecuadorean army could prepare for incursions across the border.[11] Ecuador formally supports Plan Colombia and cooperates with the United States' regional counter-narcotics effort. It granted access to U.S. aircraft on antidrug surveillance and intelligence missions to a forward operating location at the Ecuadorean air force base in Manta—an action that the FARC described as a "declaration of war."

---

[7]"Colombia's Creeping War," *Washington Post*, October 1, 2000.

[8]Echandía, pp. 48–50; "Ecuador Troops Mount Search for Kidnappers," *Financial Times*, September 15, 1999.

[9]Richard Downes, p. 4.

[10]Heinz Moeller, press conference, National Press Club, Washington, D.C., October 23, 2000.

[11]"Neighbors Worry About Colombian Aid," *New York Times*, August 25, 2000.

Nevertheless, the Ecuadoreans fear that counter-narcotics operations in southern Colombia could simply drive the drug producers and traffickers across the border into Ecuador. The Ecuadoreans point out that their armed forces gained valuable experience in jungle operations during the conflict with Peru in the Cenepa river basin in 1995, but that the military is badly in need of equipment, specifically fast river boats, helicopters, and communications and night-vision equipment.[12] Under the U.S. assistance package to Colombia and the Andean region, Ecuador is to receive $12 million for drug interdiction and $8 million for alternative agricultural development. Estimated military and police equipment requirements range between $30 and $40 million.

BRAZIL

Brazil, a rising continental power, also has an interest in controlling the activities of guerrillas, narcotraffickers, and other non-state actors across its extensive Amazonian frontiers with Colombia. Maintaining control of the border in the Amazon region is a high security priority for Brazil, but it is also a daunting challenge because of the vast distances, low population density, lack of infrastructure, and the difficulty of maintaining surveillance and stable settlements in the area.[13] Clandestine flights through Brazilian airspace are a daily occurrence and Brazilian and Colombian authorities have dismantled 16 jungle landing strips near the border.[14] Brazil's long-term response to its security dilemma in the Amazon region has been the ambitious *Sistema de Vigilencia de Amazonia* (SIVAM). Still in development, the system will have radar and airborne early warning (AEW) cover for this vast area.

The Brazilian attitude toward Plan Colombia is ambivalent, like that of other states bordering on Colombia. On the one hand, the Brasilia government would see its security interests threatened by the collapse of the Bogotá government's authority and has expressed support for Plan Colombia. On the other hand, like other neighboring

---

[12]Moeller, press conference.

[13]Edmundo Sussumo Fujita, "The Brazilian Policy of Sustainable Defense," *International Affairs*, Vol. 74, No. 3, July 1998, p. 582.

[14]"Brazil Fears Fallout of Drug Crackdown," *Washington Post*, October 1, 2000.

states of Colombia, it is concerned that the military operations associated with Plan Colombia will drive refugees, guerrillas, and drug traffickers across the border into Brazil. In September 2000, the Brazilian armed forces launched a three-year plan named Operation Cobra to increase its presence on the border with Colombia. The Brazilian government announced that it planned to deploy 6000 troops to the triple border region, where Colombia, Peru, and Brazil meet.[15]

CONCLUSIONS

Colombia's crisis has developed into a serious security concern for its neighbors. Panamanians feel helpless to prevent the use of their territory by Colombian factions. Ecuadoreans are conscious of the vulnerability of their country's vital oil installations in the Oriente, within striking distance of the Colombian border, and fear that the Colombian drug-production problem could metastasize in Ecuador. All are concerned about refugee flows from Colombia. A further deterioration of security in Colombia would pose a serious threat to the security and stability of neighboring states and drive a greater regionalization of the conflict. So far the response of most of Colombia's neighbors, as noted above, is to try to insulate themselves from the consequences of the Colombian conflict. However, efforts to control the borders are unlikely to be successful, given the remoteness and inaccessibility and the lack of government infrastructure in much of the border area.

The widening of Colombia's conflict would severely test the viability of the existing regional security architecture and of U.S. leadership in hemispheric security institutions. The states most threatened by the spillover of the conflict would seek U.S. assistance and leadership. Others could try to work out an accommodation with the guerrillas. The United States would be confronted by the choice of leading a coalition-building effort to stabilize the regional environment, letting events take their course, or deferring to initiatives led by other parties (for instance, Brazil) and accepting a commensurate loss of regional influence.

---

[15]Ibid.

Chapter Ten

IMPLICATIONS FOR U.S. INTERESTS

Which of these Colombian futures plays out will be determined by the interaction of the economic, social, political, and military trends described in the preceding chapters. Although the direction of some of these trends is not positive, the deterioration has not reached an irreversible stage (and there have been improvements in some areas, for instance, in the Colombian military's tactics and operations). Therefore, the overarching task for U.S. policy is to devise a comprehensive integrated strategy that reconciles and prioritizes counternarcotics and political-strategic objectives and reinforces Colombian government capabilities in critical areas.

If, despite these efforts, security conditions continue to deteriorate and the United States is confronted with an impending Colombian government collapse, the U.S. goal would be to ensure the survival and stability of governments in neighboring countries. The United States must work with those governments with which it has shared interests—Peru, Ecuador, Panama, and possibly Brazil and some of the Southern Cone countries—to isolate the guerrilla-controlled areas of Colombia. It could involve an increased U.S. military presence.

STRATEGIC-LEVEL CONSIDERATIONS

U.S. policy recognizes the nexus between the guerrillas and drug trafficking, but has failed to identify the political control that the guerrillas exercise over an ever-larger part of Colombia's territory and population as the center of gravity of the guerrilla/drug trafficking complex. As a result, U.S. efforts are focused on strengthening

Colombian antinarcotics capabilities while insisting that U.S. military assistance is not directed against the guerrillas. This is unrealistic, given the Colombian government's inability to eradicate the drug trade where it does not have physical control and the magnitude of the political and military threat it faces from the guerrillas and paramilitaries.

This is not to say that the struggle against drug traffickers and what Colombians call "generators of violence" could not go on simultaneously. It should, but within the framework of a comprehensive national strategy that commits the Colombian government to undertake the effort required to reverse the downside trends and reestablish the authority of the state in areas controlled or contested by nonstate actors, whether guerrillas, paramilitaries, or drug traffickers. Plan Colombia incorporates elements of a national strategy, but there is no clear link to a military strategy.[1]

The United States should reexamine the effectiveness of some of the counter-narcotics strategies that it is currently pursuing and their effects on political stability; in particular, it should review whether aerial fumigation of coca corps is the most effective means of reducing coca production at an acceptable social and political cost. Alternative strategies, such as targeting bottlenecks in the drug refining and transportation network in Colombia, should be explored.

If fumigation is considered essential, it is important to know whether fumigation efforts are linked to workable crop substitution and infrastructure development. Absent viable economic alternatives, fumigation may simply displace growers to other regions and increase support for the guerrillas.

The United States should also reexamine the utility of distinguishing between counter-narcotics and counter-insurgency assistance and consider providing assistance to improve Colombia's conventional military capabilities.

Additionally, the United States should seek to balance and integrate its own unilateral initiatives with multilateral policies that are taken

---

[1]The link is indirect: the Colombian government's assumption is that attacking the guerrillas' sources of income in the drug trade will reduce their resources and ability to prosecute the war.

in conjunction with relevant international bodies, nongovernmental organizations, and other hemispheric states.[2] Apart from these practical measures, the United States should acknowledge the critical role that American consumer demand plays in encouraging cocaine and heroin exports from Colombia and accordingly accept at least some degree of co-responsibility for the problem.

OPERATIONAL-LEVEL IMPLICATIONS

Beyond the development of a comprehensive national strategy, the Colombian government needs to develop adequate instrumentalities to implement its strategy—especially a capable military force. It would require a thoroughgoing military reform, including implementation of the Colombian High Command's goal of replacing conscripts—who currently constitute 70 percent of military personnel—with an all-volunteer force, and remedying weaknesses in mobility, intelligence, and communications.[3] The recruitment, training, and equipping of a modern and efficient military force will take substantial resources. The Colombian defense budget for the year 2000 is 3.5 percent of GDP, a level that might be appropriate for peacetime, but falls well short of what the present emergency requires.

The United States is the only realistic source of military assistance to the Colombian government on the scale needed to redress the currently unfavorable balance of power. Further assistance will be needed, beyond the $862.3 million (out of a $1.3 billion package) approved for Colombia by the U.S. Congress in 2000. The U.S. program of military assistance to El Salvador during the Reagan administration could be a relevant model. Although U.S. military assistance to El Salvador was a matter of considerable political controversy, there is no question that it succeeded in transforming the unprepossessing Salvadoran military into a force capable of turning back a formidable guerrilla threat.

---

[2]See, for instance, Shifter, "The United States and Colombia: Partners in Ambiguity," p. 55.

[3]Military Professionals Resources Inc. (MPRI), a private organization staffed by retired U.S. officers and NCOs, received a contract from the U.S. government to assist in the modernization of the Colombian armed forces. It is too early to assess the results of the MPRI work in Colombia.

Clearly, not all of the lessons of the Salvadoran war of 20 years ago are applicable to Colombia today, but some experiences apply, particularly at the operational and tactical level. The key lesson from El Salvador is the need to move forces out of static defense, to the extent possible, and remake them into mobile units to retake the initiative from the guerrillas and progressively clear them out of economically strategic areas. It would require the development of rapid reaction capabilities, including transport and attack helicopters, long-range reconnaissance assets, and intelligence collection and dissemination, particularly signals intelligence (SIGINT) for order-of-battle information.

The United States could help the Colombian military in developing new concepts of operations to detect, identify, and attack light infantry (guerrilla) targets. Air-land synergies (which the Colombian military has employed in encounters since 1998) can be an effective counter to the guerrilla tactic of massing for attack on isolated government positions or units. On-call air power can be a force multiplier, especially where the government forces on the ground can direct the fire of supporting air assets. If the guerrillas disperse to avoid the air attacks, they are vulnerable to attack by government ground forces.

Effective employment of air power against light infantry would require precise information on the type, location, and activity of the target. Newly developed sensors, weapons, and analytic tools could be well suited to the Colombian environment. Light infantry forces produce signatures that can be detected by a variety of sensors. Advances in sensor technology and data processing over the last decade make it possible to detect low-contrast targets and handle high-data-rate flows. Small unmanned aerial vehicles (UAVs) have great potential for low-altitude surveillance missions; they could be equipped with foliage-penetrating radar or other types of active or passive sensors. Another possibility is unattended ground sensors. A streamlined command and control architecture would be needed to strike targets while they are exposed.[4]

---

[4]For a detailed discussion, see Alan Vick et al., *Enhancing Air Power's Contribution Against Light Infantry Targets*, RAND, MR-697-AF, 1996.

Maintaining road control is critical to prevent the guerrillas from fragmenting the country, but it is exceptionally difficult because of Colombia's topography. The FARC has built improvised armored vehicles using bulldozers, tractors, and farm equipment. Armored vehicles for the Colombian army could be built locally, but their effective employment to keep the roads open would require air support.

More effective use of riverine and amphibious forces would be an advantageous enhancement of Colombian military capabilities. As noted above, Colombia has 18,000 kilometers of navigable rivers, the avenues of transportation in southern and southeastern Colombia. What is required is an amphibious force capable of landing and maneuvering, with naval units providing suppressing and supporting fire.[5]

Satellite communications is a critical need. Currently, the Colombian army relies for military communications on 82 relay stations throughout the country. These relay stations are resource-intensive and vulnerable to guerrilla attack. Resources could be freed, vulnerabilities reduced, and communications reliability increased by helping the Colombians shift to satellite communications for their mobile military operations.

REGIONAL COOPERATION

At the same time, the United States needs to work with concerned South American countries to contain the risk of regional destabilization. The United States should begin to explore ways of helping countries such as Panama and Ecuador regain control of their borders with Colombia.[6] Panama, as noted earlier, has become a critical node in the Colombian narcotraffickers' and guerrillas' support structure. Shutting down to the extent possible the narcotraffickers' and guerrillas' pipeline through Panama is vital to the success of any

---

[5]The authors are indebted to David Spencer for the ideas in this and the preceding paragraph.

[6]The U.S. supplemental assistance package for Colombia included modest amounts of counter-narcotics assistance for Peru ($32 million), Ecuador ($20 million), and a smaller amount for Panama.

U.S.-Colombian strategy. At the same time, the United States should help Panama fill the security vacuum in its southern province. To do that, the United States needs to help strengthen the (virtually non-existent) capabilities of the Panamanian security services. Critical requirements are the following:

- The National Police's specialized unit needs to be strengthened with heavier equipment, communications, transport, and training so it can project a more robust presence in southern Panama.

- The air service needs to develop nighttime operations, air monitoring, interceptor, and close air support capabilities. Specific requirements include radar with low-altitude capabilities; aircraft with interceptor and close air support capabilities; search and rescue equipment and training; antiterrorism equipment and training; and command, control, and intelligence improvements.

- The naval service needs landing ships for transport of personnel and amphibious operations; radar with both air and sea surveillance capabilities; fuel storage facilities at bases close to the Colombian border to extend the naval service's operational range; and specialized training for naval personnel.

Border control might be amenable to multilateral solutions. Drug production in Colombia is dependent on precursor chemicals imported from the United States, Europe, and the Southern Cone countries. Similarly, the guerrillas are dependent on an international arms pipeline. Effective multilateral cooperation to interdict the flow of precursor chemicals and to deny the arms pipeline to the guerrillas would help to reduce the size of the problem. This effort will require strengthening the defense and interdiction capabilities of neighboring countries, especially Panama and Ecuador.

The inter-American community should also begin to explore a regional response to the possible spread of Colombia's war beyond its borders. The Speaker of the Panamanian legislature suggested the deployment of an international military force to southern Panama. Although such a deployment might be premature, the United States should actively pursue all avenues of regional defense cooperation and lay the groundwork for a multilateral response if the crisis in

Colombia intensifies and threatens the stability of neighboring countries.

CONCLUSIONS

In the end, for the United States to address effectively the multiple crises in Colombia would require a conceptual shift. For the last decade Colombia has been viewed in the United States through the prism of the drug problem and counter-narcotics policy, but as this report has documented, the development of a drug economy in Colombia is inextricably linked to other factors of political and social disintegration. Strengthening the state and its institutions, including the armed and security forces—which bear the brunt of the struggle to reestablish the state's authority—should be a critical focus of U.S. policy toward Colombia. It is also important to recognize that the United States has broader strategic interests in the region that are endangered by Colombia's instability. A proactive U.S. policy would help the Colombians gradually to reduce the scope of the drug and insurgency problem; the policy should at the same time have a strong hedging element and lay the groundwork for a multilateral response if the crisis in Colombia intensifies.

THE COLOMBIAN ARMED FORCES

MILITARY REFORM

The defeats suffered by Colombian military forces in 1997 and 1998 convinced the government of the need to strengthen and modernize the military. In the view of Colombian analysts, the military high command under General Tapias has become more self-critical and open to change than in the past.[1] In 1999 and 2000, significant changes included:

A new vision of operations, with emphasis on mobility and rapid reaction, improvement of the collection and processing of information, and development of an integrated communications system. After Mitu, which was overrun by FARC guerrillas in 1998, in particular, the military has learned to integrate air power in support of ground operations.

Development of a rapid deployment capability. The three mobile brigades (that previously were not, in fact, mobile because they lacked air transport and were assigned to territorial defense) have been consolidated with the special forces brigade into a Rapid Deployment Force. The Colombian military, for the first time, now has a striking force of some 4000, all professional soldiers who can be deployed anywhere in the country. The main constraint on the Rapid Reaction Force is insufficient air transport assets.

---

[1]Interview with Rangel.

Improvements in the employment of air power. In addition to better-integrated operations with the land forces, the air force is now able to conduct night operations using night-vision equipment.

Improvements in intelligence collection. Better training and equipment has provided the Colombian military with improved signals intelligence (SIGINT). Human intelligence (HUMINT), a critical factor, remains difficult to remedy in guerrilla areas because of the guerrillas' familiarity with the terrain and network of social control.

Efforts to inculcate respect for human rights and customary international humanitarian law. Members of the military and the police at all levels receive an average of 90 hours a year in training in human rights and international humanitarian law.[2] The Colombian government has brought to justice officers and NCOs accused of complicity in human rights violations.[3]

The new operational and tactical approaches of the Colombian military have produced some results, as noted in Chapter Four. However, there is a need for caution in reaching any conclusions. The military situation remains dynamic and there is not enough evidence that the military can control the guerrillas. The Colombian military has the advantage in numbers and firepower, but the guerrillas maintain the operational and tactical initiative. In the majority of encounters, the guerrillas choose the time and place of attack. In Vigía del Fuente, Chocó, in March–April 2000, and in Arboleda, Caldas, in August 2000, the guerrillas attacked and destroyed fortified police posts, while the army was unable to send reinforcements in time to save the besieged police units.

Moreover, the ability of guerrillas to adjust should not be underestimated. In the case of El Salvador, the FMLN adjusted to the increased mobility and air power of the Salvadoran military by introducing portable surface-to-air missiles, making greater use of an-

---

[2]*La fuerza pública y los derechos humanos en Colombia,* p. 27.

[3]Colombian officers point out that in almost all the cases the accusations regard acts of omission, that is, failing to prevent killings by irregular forces in their area of responsibility rather than active participation in these incidents. The question is whether the commanders responsible for areas where atrocities occurred lacked the means or opportunity to prevent the incidents (as some of the accused claim), chose to ignore them, or abetted the perpetrators.

tipersonnel mines, and scaling down the size of their military formations.[4] They also moved from mobile to intense attrition warfare.[5]
Given the importance of air in Colombian military strategy, the use
of surface-to-air missiles by the guerrillas could change the strategic
balance by forcing the Colombian military to curtail air operations
and rely on land transport for troop movements.

FORCE POSTURE

At this writing, about one third of the Colombian military's 144,000
total strength is in training or defending fixed installations. Another
13 percent are defending 842 critical infrastructure points, such as
bridges, roads, the communications network, oil and electrical
installations, and airports. Some 5 percent are deployed as border
guards. This leaves somewhat less than half of the standing force
available for operations.[6]

The new doctrine emphasizes mobility and a shift from a defensive
to an offensive posture. To implement Plan Colombia's counter-
narcotics military component, the army is creating three new
counter-narcotics battalions that are at the heart of the Plan's military component. The new counter-narcotics battalions will be more
proficient than the regular battalions, but will also present more lucrative targets for the guerrillas.

At the same time, the guerrillas' attacks on small towns and isolated
police stations are increasing the army's requirement to provide
static defense. According to Colombian military figures, there is an
unmet requirement for police and military protection of 254 *municipios* and *corregimientos*, one fourth of the total number.[7]

MOBILITY

Mobility is the key to the Colombian military strategy. Only by being
able to bring reinforcements rapidly can the Colombian military

---

[4]Steve Salisbury, "Guerras diferentes," *Semana,* September 13, 2000.

[5]Personal communication from David Spencer, December 2000.

[6]Colombian armed forces briefing, April 2000.

[7]Ibid.

neutralize the guerrillas' operational and tactical advantages. Mobility means air transport, because the guerrillas are able to mine the roads (where they exist) that military convoys must traverse to reach threatened points. Yet, to cover a country of 1.4 million square kilometers and 6,322 kilometers of territorial borders, the Colombian military has only 25 heavy transport helicopters, of which 17 are operational.[8]   U.S. assistance to Plan Colombia provides an additional 30 UH-60 Black Hawk and 33 UH-1H Huey transport helicopters, yet to be delivered. Use of these assets, however, is restricted to counter-narcotics operations. After the bloody FARC attack on the Arboleda police outpost in July 2000, the U.S. Embassy in Bogotá was obliged to defend the Colombians' use of U.S.-provided helicopters to reach the outpost by arguing that they could be used to defend government forces under attack in an area where there were counter-narcotics activities.[9]

RECRUITMENT

The Colombian armed forces have a professional component, currently 30.9 percent of the force. The remaining 69.1 percent are draftees who serve for 12 to 18 months. Of this number, 50.1 percent have not completed high school, and 19.0 percent are *bachilleres*, or high-school graduates.[10]   However, according to Colombian law, high school graduates are exempted from combat duty. As a result, draftees from lower-class sectors of society have borne the brunt of the fighting, introducing an invidious element of class privilege into the Colombian government's military effort.

As General Tapias explained in a conversation with one of the authors, the Colombian military's goal is to move to a 50 percent volunteer force by 2001, and eventually to an all-volunteer force.[11] This will also require improvements in the quality of life, level of education, and training and evaluation methods. The problem, as with the

---

[8]Colombian armed forces briefing, April 2000.

[9]"Colombian Rebels Besiege Town," *New York Times,* July 31, 2000.

[10]Colombian armed forces briefing, April 2000.

[11]Conversation with General Tapias, Bogotá, April 2000.

rest of the military's professionalization and modernization plans, is whether the resources are available for implementation.

MILITARY BUDGET

The budget for Colombia's military and police is 4500 billion pesos (U.S. $2.5 billion at an exchange rate of 1820 pesos to the dollar). As a proportion of GDP (3.56 percent), the amount allocated to defense and security has not changed substantially over the past decade, as shown in Table A.1. Although Colombian military and police expenditures as a proportion of GDP are higher than the average for Latin America, such a level of expenditures is nevertheless low for a country fighting an active insurgency.

Table A.1

Colombian Defense Budget

Year	Funding (in millions of pesos)	Percentage of GDP
1990	367,139	2.34
1991	467,931	2.29
1992	701,737	2.69
1993	1,104,292	3.23
1994	1,296,202	3.11
1995	1,774,994	3.44
1996	2,500,085	3.59
1997	3,328,106	3.89
1998	3,756,476	3.59
1999	4,437,311	4.03
2000	4,501,706	3.56

SOURCE: Colombian Ministry of Defense.

BIBLIOGRAPHY

BOOKS

Amnesty International, *Annual Reports, Colombia,* 1997–2000.

Arnson, Cynthia J., *Comparative Peace Processes in Latin America,* Woodrow Wilson Center Press, Washington, D.C., 1999.

Arquilla, John, and David Ronfeldt (eds.), *In Athena's Camp: Preparing for Conflict in the Information Age,* RAND, MR-880-OSD/RGI, 1997

_____, *The Advent of Netwar,* RAND, MR-789-OSD, 1996.

Australian Bureau of Criminal Intelligence, *Australian Illicit Drug Report 1997–98,* Canberra, 1998.

Bushnell, David, *The Making of Modern Colombia: A Nation in Spite of Itself,* University of California Press, Berkeley, 1993.

Davies, John L., and Ted Robert Gurr (eds.), *Preventive Measures: Building Risk Assessment and Crisis Early Warning Systems,* Rowman and Littlefield Publishing Group, Lanham, Maryland, 1998.

Echandía Castilla, Camilo, *El Conflicto Armado y las Manifestaciones de la Violencia en las Regiones de Colombia,* Presidencia de la República de Colombia, Oficina del Alto Comisionado para la Paz, Bogotá, 2000.

Europa World Year Book, "Colombia," Europa Publications, London, 1999.

Fals Borda, Orlando, *Subversion and Social Change in Colombia,* Columbia University Press, New York, 1969.

Garay S., Jorge Luis, *Globalización y crisis,* Tercer Mundo Editores/ Colciencias, Bogotá, 1999.

Garay S., Jorge Luis, et al., *Colombia: estructura industrial e internacionalización, 1967–1996,* Tomo I, República de Colombia, Departamento Nacional de Planeación, Bogotá, 1998.

Graham, Bob, Brent Scowcroft, and Michael Shifter, *Toward Greater Peace and Security in Colombia: Forging a Constructive U.S. Policy,* Task Force Report, Council on Foreign Relations, New York, 2000.

International Institute of Strategic Studies (IISS), "International Drug Trade," *Strategic Survey,* 1997/98, Oxford University Press, London, 1998.

Khalilzad, Zalmay M., John P. White, and Andrew W. Marshall, *Strategic Appraisal: The Changing Role of Information in Warfare,* RAND, MR-1016-AF, 1999.

Leal Buitrago, Francisco, *El oficio de la guerra,* Tercer Mundo Editores, Bogotá, 1994.

Martz, John D., *The Politics of Clientelism: Democracy and the State in Colombia,* Transaction Publishers, New Brunswick, New Jersey, and London, 1997.

Maullin, Richard, *Soldiers, Guerrillas, and Politics in Colombia,* RAND, R-0630-ARPA, 1971.

Oquist, Paul, *Conflict and Politics in Colombia,* Academic Press, New York, 1980.

Pizarro, Eduardo, *Insurgencia sin revolución,* Tercer Mundo Editores, Bogotá, 1996.

Rangel Suárez, Alfredo, *Colombia: guerra en el fin de siglo,* Tercer Mundo Editores, Bogotá, 1998.

Ronfeldt, David, John Arquilla, Graham E. Fuller, and Melissa Fuller, *The Zapatista Social Netwar in Mexico*, RAND, MR-994-A, 1998.

Santos Calderón, Enrique, *Fuego Cruzado: Guerrilla, Narcotráfico y Paramilitares en la Colombia de los Ochentos*, CEREC, Bogotá, 1989.

United States Commission on National Security/21st Century, *New World Coming: American Security in the 21st Century*, Phase I Report on the Emerging Global Security Environment for the First Quarter of the 21st Century, September 15, 1999.

Vick, Alan, John Bordeaux, David Orletsky, and David A. Shlapak, *Enhancing Air Power's Contribution Against Light Infantry Targets*, RAND, MR-697-AF, 1996.

Zackrison, James L. (ed.), *Crisis: What crisis? Security Issues in Colombia*, Institute for National Strategic Studies (INSS), National Defense University, Washington, D.C., 1999.

ARTICLES AND PAPERS

Bagley, Bruce M., "The Evolution of Drug Trafficking in Colombia in the 1990s," unpublished paper provided to authors, February 2000.

Center for International Policy, *The Content of the Colombia Aid Package*, in www.ciponline.org/colombia/aid/aidsumm.htm.

Chalk, Peter, "Heroin and Cocaine: A Global Threat," *Jane's Intelligence Review*, January 6, 1998.

Collier, Paul, and Anke Hoeffler, "Justice-Seeking and Loot-Seeking in Civil War," paper presented at the World Bank Workshop on "Civil Conflicts, Crime and Violence in Developing Countries," 1999.

Colombia, República de, Ministerio de Defensa Nacional, *La fuerza pública y los derechos humanos en Colombia*, Bogotá, March 2000.

Colombia, Republic of, *Plan Colombia: Plan for Peace, Prosperity, and the Strengthening of the State*, Presidency of the Republic of Colombia, Bogotá, October 1999 edition.

Downes, Richard, *Landpower and Ambiguous Warfare: The Challenge of Colombia in the 21st Century,* Strategic Studies Institute (SSI) Conference Report, March 10, 1999.

Fuerzas Armadas Revolucionarias de Colombia (FARC), "Las FARC: 30 años de lucha por la paz, democracia y soberanía," in http://tierra.ucsd.edu/farc-ep/Nuestra_historia/.

Fujita, Edmundo Sussumo, "The Brazilian Policy of Sustainable Defense," *International Affairs,* Vol. 74, No. 3, July 1998.

Geopolitical Drug Watch, "A Drug Primer for the Late 1990s," *Current History,* 97/618, 1998.

González, Libardo, "El Plan Colombia: una paz armada," *Colombia Thema,* No. 7, March–May 2000, in http://www.colombia-thema.org.

Grassley, Sen. Charles, "The U.S. Effort to Fight Drug Abuse" *Global Issues* 2/3, June 1997.

Marcella, Gabriel, and Donald Schulz, *Colombia's Three Wars: U.S. Strategy at the Crossroads,* Strategic Studies Institute (SSI), United States Army War College, Carlisle Barracks, March 5, 1999.

Passage, David, "Colombia's Struggle," *Adelante,* Summer 2000.

Penhaul, Karl, "Colombian Rebels Map Out Plan to Topple Government," News Agency Colombia, January 14, 1999.

Perafán, Carlos César, "Impacto de cultivos ilícitos en pueblos indígenas: el caso de Colombia," Banco Interamericano de Desarrollo (BID), Washington, D.C., 1999.

Posada, Miguel, "Colombia's Illegal Self-Defense Groups," Centro de Información sobre el Desarrollo de la Democracia en Colombia (CIDEC), February 1998, in www.cidec.org.

Rubio, Mauricio, "La violencia en Colombia: dimensionamiento y políticas de control," Serie de documentos de trabajo R-345, Inter-American Development Bank, Washington, D.C., October 1998.

Shifter, Michael, "Colombia at War," *Current History,* 98/626, 1999.

Shifter, Michael, "The United States and Colombia: Partners in Ambiguity," *Current History*, 99/634, 2000.

Spencer, David, "FARC Warfare Strategy and Tactics 1996–1999," unpublished manuscript.

Spencer, David, and Heather Noss, *Colombia: Strategic End State, Goals, and Means: A Workshop Report*, Center for Strategic Studies, The CNA Corporation, Arlington, Virginia, November 2000.

Tickner, Arlene, "Colombia: Chronicle of a Crisis Foretold," *Current History*, 97/616, 1998.

U.S. Congressional Research Service, "Colombia: The Problem of Illegal Narcotics and U.S.-Colombian Relations," March 1998.

U.S. Department of State, Bureau for International Narcotics and Law Enforcement Affairs, *International Narcotics Control Strategy Report, 1999*, Washington, D.C., 2000.

U.S. Federal Bureau of Investigation, *Supplementary Homicide Reports, 1976–1998*, accessed via http://www.oip.usdoj.gov/bjs/homicide/city.htm.

U.S. House of Representatives, Government Reform Committee, Criminal Justice, Drug Policy and Human Resources Subcommittee, Testimony by William Ledwith, Chief of the Drug Enforcement Agency International Operations, Washington, D.C., February 15, 2000.

Williams, Phil, "The Nature of Drug-Trafficking Networks," *Current History*, 97/618, 1998.

World Bank, "Local Government Capacity in Colombia: Beyond Technical Assistance," Washington, D.C., 1995.

World Bank, "Violence in Colombia: Building Sustainable Peace and Social Capital," Washington, D.C., 2000.

Youngers, Coletta, "U.S. Entanglements in Colombia Continue," *Report of the Americas, The Wars Within: Counterinsurgency in Chiapas and Colombia*, Vol. 31, No. 5, March/April 1998.

Zirnite, Peter, "The Militarization of the Drug War in Latin America," *Current History,* 97/618, 1998.

NEWSPAPERS AND PERIODICALS

Cambio (Bogotá)

Colombia Thema (Bogotá)

Colombia Update (Colombia Human Rights Network)

The Economist

El Espectator (Bogotá)

El Tiempo (Bogotá)

El Universal (Caracas)

Financial Times

The Independent

New York Times

Semana (Bogotá)

Venezuela Analítica

Wall Street Journal

Washington Post

Washington Times

OTHER SOURCES

In addition to published materials, the research relied on field work in Venezuela, Colombia, and Panama in April 2000. The authors interviewed the commandant and members of the staff of the Institute of Higher Defense Studies of Venezuela; the commander of the armed forces of Colombia; and the director of the National Police, the deputy directors of the Panamanian air and naval services, and other officials in the security services of Panama. We also interviewed Colombian, Venezuelan, and Panamanian political practitioners and defense analysts, and U.S. experts on Colombia. For the effects of the armed conflict at the local level, we are indebted to the organizers of the Georgetown University and National Endowment for Democracy Conference on "Local Government Amidst the Armed Conflict: The Experience of Colombian Mayors," Georgetown University, Washington, D.C., September 27, 2000, which brought together mayors from 11 Colombian cities and towns and officials from the Colombian Federation of Municipalities and the Federation of Municipal Councils. There was also valuable material applicable to the violence in Colombia presented at the World Bank's Workshop on "Civil Conflict, Crime, and Violence in Developing Countries," Washington, D.C., February 22–23, 1999. Finally, there is a great deal of useful material on the Internet, including the Web sites of some of the key players, such as the Colombian armed forces, the Revolutionary Armed Forces of Colombia, the National Liberation Army, and the major Colombian political parties.